JESUS HIS MIRACLES

FRED TREXLER, JR.

ISBN 0-9644030-0-5

Library of Congress Catalog Card Number: 95-68060

Destiny Press
A Division of Minutes of Destiny, Inc.
P.O. Box 431
Cordova, TN 38088-0431

Produced by JM Productions, Brentwood, Tennessee
PRINTED IN THE UNITED STATES OF AMERICA

Contents

Introduction..v

1. Wine for a Wedding
   (Miracle at Cana)...1

2. The Unclean Clean
   (Lepers Healed)...9

3. No Distance in Prayer
   (Centurion's Servant) 15

4. The Touch of Faith
   (Woman Afflicted for Twelve Years)........................21

5. Healing at Home
   (Peter's Mother-in-Law) 27

6. Winds and Water
   (Sea Calmed)...31

7. Full of Devils
   (The Man with an Unclean Spirit)..........................35

8. A Meal for the Multitudes
   (Five Thousand Fed) 41

9. Walking on Water
   (Jesus Walking on the Sea) 47

10. A Faith Rewarded
    (The Syrophenician's Daughter)...........................51

11. The Great Catch
    (Draught of Fishes) 55

12. A Cripple Cured
    (An Impotent Man Healed).................................61

13. Delivered from Death
    (Raising of Lazarus) 65

Conclusion 75

Footnotes...83

Bibliography...89

Introduction

If we are to begin an understanding of Jesus' miracles at all, we must view them against the mental and spiritual climate of the age in which they were performed. Since that is the case, certain facts about the New Testament era have to be taken into account.

People in that day had a completely different attitude toward the miraculous. Many modern men are suspicious of the miraculous as well; they dislike whatever they cannot explain, and they think that they know so much about the universe and its workings that they can claim that miracles do not occur. Most moderns do not expect a miracle. On the other hand, the ancient world reveled in the miraculous. It looked for miracles; it expected miracles; and the result was the miraculous events happened. [1]

We must consider still another characteristic of the Hebrew mind. The Hebrew seldom or never thought of matters, or explained events, in terms of what we would call secondary causes. We would state that certain atmospheric conditions caused the thunder, the lightning or the rain; the Hebrew would simply state that God sent the thunder, the lightning, or the rain. We would claim that certain weather conditions caused the failure of crops. The Hebrew would explain that God sent blasting and mildew and caused a famine.

There was also a belief in Jesus' day that sin and suffering were linked together. The Jews believed that there could be no suffering without some sin to account for it, and that there could be no sin without some suffering to ensue from it.

In seeking to understand the miracles of Jesus I believe there is also one other factor to mull over. It is obvious that we cannot view anything as someone else does, unless we see it from his standpoint and from his slant. With the single exception of Luke all the New Testament writers were Jews; they, therefore, interpreted events through Jewish eyes. If, then, we try to comprehend their writings in terms of modern Western thought we are bound to distort them. When we perceive them from their perspective, we confront one consistent principle of Jewish writing and teaching. No Jewish teacher would ask of any story: "Did this literally happen?" He would ask: "What does this teach?" This is to indicate that Jewish teachers were more concerned with truth than with fact.[2]

The Greek words used for the miracles of Jesus are in themselves expressive of the character and the nature of the miracles. Three words are employed for the miracles in the New Testament.

The miracles are called *dunameis*, which means "works of power" (Matt. 11:20-23, 13:54,58; Mark 6:2,5; Luke 10:13, 19:37). It is written of Jesus that the power (*dunameis*) of the Lord was with Him to heal (Luke 5:17). It is further stated that power (*dunameis*) came forth from Him, and He healed them all (Luke 6:19). And this was a power of which Jesus was conscious, for, when He was touched in the crowd by the woman with the issue of blood, He was conscious that power had gone out of him (Mark 5:30; Luke 8:46). From this word we learn that the miracles are the result of divine power into the human situation for help and healing.

The word *teras* is utilized to describe the miracles, but it is never used alone. *Teras* means that which produces wonder, amazement, and astonishment.

When *teras* is used, it is along with *semeion*, meaning "a sign." In Acts Jesus' miracles are declared to be signs and wonders (2:22), and signs and wonders were frequent phenomena in the life of the early church (Acts 2:43, 4:30, 5:12, 6:8, 14:3, 15:12). *Semeion* is the characteristic word for the miracles of Jesus in the fourth Gospel, although it is not used in the Synoptics (John 2:11,23, 3:2, 4:54, 6:2, 7:31, 9:16, 11:47, 12:18, 20:30).

Semeion is the word which really describes the miracles of Jesus. It represents a sign, a significant event, an action which reveals the mind and character of the person who performs it. It is an outward action designed to allow him who sees it to have insight into the inner mind and heart of Him who performs it. Above all, the miracles were events which revealed the mind and heart of Jesus, and through Him the mind and heart of God.[3]

Analysis in terms of religious history requires us to recognize the Gospel accounts of miracles as historically valid. The miracles recounted in the oldest traditions are those of revelation, in which the divine glory and the brotherly humanity of Jesus are manifested.[4]

What is the purpose of the miracles? Naturally, a primary purpose was to reveal the divine nature of God in the person of Jesus Christ. The fact that only God could accomplish what Jesus did gave testimony and proof to His claim to being "the Son of God."

They are also the revelation of two other factors. They are, as we have already seen, the revelation of power. In them we behold in action a power which is able to deal with the human situation, a power through which pain and suffering can be defeated, a power through which sin, and its consequences, can be overcome. They are the revelation of pity. How characteristic of Jesus that He was "moved with compassion," either for the crowds or for an individual sufferer. The word is *splagchnizesthai*, which is the strongest word in Greek for the experience of pity and compassion. *Splagchna* are the "bowels, the viscera, the inner being," and the word describes the pity and compassion which move a person to the depths of his being. The miracles, therefore, are the signs of power and pity in the heart of Jesus, and therefore in the heart of God. They are the signs that God cares, and that God can make His care effective. They are the signs that the power of God is used in pity, and that the pity of God is backed by power. In the miracles we watch the power and the compassion of God combine to deal with the needs of the individual.[5]

The miracles of Jesus give meaning and foundation to the whole framework of the Gospel story. Crowds flocked to Jesus for the help and healing which He alone could give them. Naturally, not everyone in Jesus' day was healed. Every blind person did not receive sight. Every deaf person did not gain hearing ability. Every lame person did not walk. Every person who died was not resurrected. However, Jesus did not refuse to meet the needs of those who asked for His help and healing. In fact, there is not one single instance where Jesus refused to heal a person who needed it and requested it.

Jesus declared: "the thief cometh not, but for to steal, and to kill, and to destroy: I am come that they might have life, and that they might have it more abundantly" (John 10:10).

1
WINE FOR A WEDDING
Miracle at Cana

And the third day there was a marriage in Cana of Galilee: and the mother of Jesus was there: And both Jesus was called, and his disciples, to the marriage. And when they wanted wine, the mother of Jesus saith unto him, They have no wine. Jesus saith unto her, Woman, what have I to do with thee? Mine hour is not yet come. His mother saith unto the servants, Whatsoever he saith unto you, do it. And there was set there six waterpots of stone, after the manner of the purifying of the Jews, containing two or three firkins apiece. Jesus saith unto them, Fill the waterpots with water. And they filled them up to the brim. And he saith unto them, Draw out now, and bear unto the governor of the feast. And they bare it. When the ruler of the feast had tasted the water that was made wine, and knew not whence it was: (but the servants which drew the water knew;) the governor of the feast called the bridegroom, and saith unto him, Every man at the beginning doth set forth good wine; and when men have well drunk, then that which is worse: but thou hast kept the good wine until now. This beginning of miracles did Jesus in Cana of Galilee, and manifested forth his glory: and his disciples believed on him (John 2:1-11).

Analysis and Word Study

1. *The third day.* The third day from the start to Galilee when Phillip was found (1:43), seven days since 1:19.[1]

There was a marriage. A wedding or marriage festival (see Matt. 22:2,8). In Palestine a wedding was a very important occasion.

Jewish law required the wedding of a virgin to take place on Wednesday. In Palestine, wedding festivities lasted more than a day.[2]

Cana of Galilee. This town, the home of Nathanael (21:2), is mentioned again only in 4:46 as the home of the nobleman. There was a Cana in Coele-Syria. It is located about three miles from Nazareth at Kefr Kenna.[3]

Mother of Jesus. John never mentions her name. Probably Joseph was already dead.[4]

Was there. When they arrived. She was probably a close friend of the family, assisting in the preparations.[5]

2. *Jesus was called, and His disciples* means He was bidden. This could refer to the five whose calling has just been recorded, Andrew and Peter, Philip and Nathanael, and John.[6] They came because they were with Jesus.

3. *They wanted wine.* It was an embarrassing circumstance, especially to Mary. It could have happened because of the extra guests. It is not easy to determine exactly what she expected. Mary seems to have felt responsible for remedying the situation. She had experienced His wonders through the years since His birth.[8]

4. *Woman.* The word woman (*gunai*) is somewhat misleading. There is no disrespect here. It does imply the independence on the part of Jesus from His mother when necessary. When Jesus spoke to Mary, He was simply telling her to leave matters to Him.[9] It is a highly respectful and affectionate kind of address. Compare with 22:13,15.[10]

What have I to do with thee? (*Tiemoi kai soi*) Literally, the phrase means, "What it is to me and to thee?" Examples of this are found in Mark 1:24, 5:7, Matt. 8:29, 27:19, Luke 8:28).[11]

Expositors of the early church have found in these words an element of reproof and repulsion. Roman Catholics admit the appearance of such; only they deny the reality. It does teach a higher duty involved in the decisions manifesting His ministry.[12]

Mine hour is not yet come. Compare this with John 8:20, 12:23, 13:1. In each case the coming of the hour indicates some crisis in the personal life of the Lord. Here it is the hour of His Messianic manifestation (v. 11).[13]

2

5. *Unto the servants (tois diakonois.)* See Matt. 20:26, Mark 9:35.

Whatsoever he saith unto you, do it. Mary apparently recognized the independence of Jesus but still expected Him to do what she wanted.[15]

6. *Six waterpots of stone.* An old word from *hudor* (water) and used in papyri for pots or pans for holding money or bread, as well as water. These stone pots were made available at a feast for ceremonial cleansing of the hands (Mark 7:3).[16]

After the manner of the purifying of the Jews, containing two or three firkins apiece. The purifications customary among the Jews. The words denote space or room for holding something. Firkins—a liquid measure containing nearly nine gallons.[17]

7. *Fill the waterpots with water, up to the brim.* They filled them to the very top. No room was left in the waterpots.[18]

8. *"Draw out now and bear to the governor of the feast."* This occurs in John 4:7,15 for drawing water from the well. This was taken from the waterpots—not from the well. The water was still water when it came out of the jars but was changed to wine before reaching the guests.[19]

The governor could mean a servant or someone designated to have charge, a wine steward. It most likely meant one of the guests who was supervising the occasion. The Greek and Roman customs support this view. He was in charge of tasting and distributing the wine. Jesus honored this custom by having the wine given to him first.[20]

9. *Tasted the water that was made wine.* The water was now wine. When did it become wine? Robertson states the water was still water when it came out of the jars but was changed to wine before reaching the ruler.[21] This would mean only the amount used would represent wine. It is possible that all the water in the waterpots was wine.

10. *Have well drunk.* They have drunk enough to be satisfied with the taste and quality of the wine. The verb here does not mean that the guests were drunk, but that a common custom has been followed to put "the worst" (the inferior) wine last. Jesus mingled

3

in the social life of the time and was even criticized for it (Matt. 11:19, Luke 7:34). However, this fact does not mean that today Jesus would approve of the modern liquor trade or the drinking habits of many people.[22]

11. *This beginning of miracles.* The correct word is signs rather than wonders (*terata*) or powers (*dunameis*) (see Matt. 11:20, 24:24). There was more than a marvelous event. It was a sign. Jesus, unlike John the Baptist, began His ministry with a miracle.[23]

Interpretation and Application

Jesus, His mother, and His disciples attended a marriage in Cana, a village near Nazareth. A marriage like this would usually be conducted in the middle of the week. The actual ceremony occurred late at night. Afterwards, the couple went home for their honeymoon. They took the long way around so the people could wish them well on their new journey in life.[25] Their customs differed vastly from ours. The bride's family had to furnish a sizable dowry, and the groom's family was responsible for all the social activity. It was a time of joy and thanksgiving.

Torches were lighted at night to meet the groom with singers and musicians. The house was filled with food, with wineskins full of wine, with laughter, light, and music. The peasants felt rich. However, for the man who, because of his means or lack of them, seldom sees cause for spending lavishly, who never eats and drinks and entertains as much as he would like, the day of his wedding is the greatest event in his life.

It is a brilliant sunrise that dispels all the clouds of his dull, drab, commonplace existence. Unlike the wealthy people who can have banquets and entertain frequently, those who consume in a day or night what would have sufficed for a week or more for the poor man, to whom such an occasion is merely one among many. For the peasant, the poor, the villager, who lives each day on the simple food, bread, fish, figs, and on occasion killing the lamb or the kid, for the young man who has had to do without, to live with the needed instead of the wanted things, this is truly a special event, the event of events.[26] It is the highest fulfillment of his years spent on earth. All of life is centered around the bride and groom.

There was a social class structure in Jesus' day. However, this wedding party did not fit into the higher-society set. Mary was simply a peasant woman and most likely, so were the girl and boy of Cana.

The family had run out of wine. In that day and time such an incident would have been a source of embarrassment to the host. Mary brought this matter to the attention of Jesus because she knew His power. She must have witnessed many unusual facets about Jesus as He grew up, and she knew that He could take care of the situation. Jesus said to her, "Woman, what have I to do with thee? Mine hour is not yet come" (John 2:4). The word "woman" here is the same as that used by Jesus on the cross when He spoke to Mary: "Woman, behold thy son" (John 19:26). He spoke tenderly to his mother about the fact that it was not really time for Him to demonstrate His power before people.[27]

She did not, however, hesitate to tell the servants: "Whatsoever he saith unto you, do it" (John 2:5). There was always plenty of water present in the Jewish household, even though they did not have running water. There were six waterpots available. Jesus instructed them, " 'Fill the waterpots with water,' and they filled them up to the brim. And he saith unto them, 'Draw out now, and bear unto the governor of the feast,' and they bare it. When the ruler of the feast had tasted the water that was made wine, and knew not whence it was: (but the servants which drew the water knew); the governor of the feast called the bridegroom, and saith unto him, 'Every man at the beginning doth set forth good wine; and when men have well drunk, then that which is worse: but thou hast kept the good wine until now" (John 2:7-10).

Some people simply cannot cope with a miracle. So, they rationalize that somehow Jesus had some wine brought to the occasion as a present or that a higher truth is being taught such as: the blessings of Jesus are inexhaustible. These pseudo-intellectuals miss the entire target by not aiming at the bullseye.

It occurred literally as it reads—the power of God over matter. He who created water in the first place can certainly change it into wine. The Lord of heaven and salvation not only wishes to save men's lives from hell but also desires to help them with everyday needs on earth.

5

How wise it is to do what Jesus asks us to do. If we could only know the wish, the will, and the command of our Lord in each action, we would always make the right decision. It is important to be surrendered to His will, to be obedient. His way of life is the best life possible here and hereafter. The best wine was usually given to the guests first and the worst, later. What a surprise when the best wine was served last. Since Jesus always provides the best, why do we not trust Him? Why do we not seek Him? Why do we not surrender to His will? When we do, we, too, will be surprised at what He can and will do with us.

Wine, in some countries, is the primary drink made available. Jesus drank it with the Twelve before His death, symbolic of His blood shed on Calvary.

What a sad commentary that some have adopted this one incident at Cana to create a ridiculous license to drink, become drunk, and participate in the kind of offensive activity that has absolutely nothing to do with the miracle at Cana.

The new wine replaced the old. Who would want the old sour, unripened wine, the poorer quality, symbolic of the old law, the old covenant?[28] Our sins are simply trash to be discarded, our feeble minds are so limited in understanding; our lives are filled with the sourness of worry, frustration, doubt, and despair. Jesus offers us the new wine of wisdom and understanding. It is the new law, the new covenant, the new way of salvation and righteousness. It is a doorway to heaven, but also a highway of hope for each day.

Jesus often talked of weddings and banquets. The parable of the king who sent invitations to the wedding of his son, and another of the virgins who waited by night for the arrival of the bridegroom's friends, and also of the Lord who prepared a banquet. Christ compared Himself to a bridegroom given a feast by his friends upon answering those who are offended because His disciples ate and drank.

Jesus enjoyed weddings because he liked to watch people having a good time. Many folks miss the whole point and purpose of following the Master. It is to have the most exciting, exhilarating, active, fun-filled time possible. Some people equate a union with Jesus as the worst possible misery, the saddest life, the most boring experience possible. They are wrong. If they knew Him, they would know better. If they experienced Him, they would raise a banner for His cause. If they served Him, they would recognize that He, indeed, serves the very best wine of life—His life.

Jesus was happy for those simple souls who, for a few hours and a few days, were lifted above their everyday existence to a festival of fun. Jesus recognized more than a festival here: He saw two lives coming together, two hearts combined, two bodies united. It was the joining of two young people into a oneness that only marriage can produce: two loves, two affections, two hopes, two hostages held captive by vows, pledges, promises, commitments. The marriage partners had pledged themselves to a bond of blessing, for marriage is a blessing, a promise of happiness, and an acceptance of suffering. Marriage is at once a reality and a dilemma which separate from parental ties. It demands new responsibilities and many sacrifices.

We need a new miracle for each marriage today. The foundation for marriage that seems present before and during the ceremony is too easily shattered upon the modern rocks of disillusionment, despair, and disaster.

No one understands marriage better than Jesus. He created it in the garden of Eden. Whom God hath joined, let no man put asunder. Man put away his wife in Moses' day because of the hardness of his heart, but Jesus taught that from the beginning it was not so. God planned for permanence in marriage, "until death do us part." Life on earth is changing, weak, and failing. Jesus is the unchanging Christ, the strong Savior, and the faithful Lord, who holds out His arms to every married couple who will come into His embrace for security and shelter.

"This beginning of miracles did Jesus in Cana of Galilee, and manifested forth his glory; and his disciples believed on Him" (John 2:11). We will always find a threefold reason for the miracles of Jesus. *First, God is glorified.* The power of God is manifested for all to see and know that the Lord is God. *Second, to meet a personal need, for Jesus cares about people.* He came to meet their needs. *Third, when a miracle occurs, it causes someone to believe.* In this case, His disciples found faith in Jesus. It helped them to realize His power. It helped them to have confidence in the person to whom they had committed their lives. It will help you, too. Ask God today to meet a special need in your life. Ask Him if there is anything He

7

wants you to do with your life. When He answers, do whatever He suggests. Watch for His answer to your need and expect it. When it comes, thank Him for it. He is alive and wants to help you, even if it requires a miracle to do so.

2
THE UNCLEAN CLEAN
Lepers Healed

And it came to pass, as he went to Jerusalem, that he passed through the midst of Samaria and Galilee. And as he entered into a certain village, there met him ten men that were lepers, which stood afar off; and they lifted up their voices, and said, Jesus, Master, have mercy on us. When he saw them, he said unto them, go shew yourselves unto the priests. And it came to pass, that, as they went, they were cleansed. And one of them, when he saw that he was healed, turned back, and with a loud voice glorified God, and fell down on his face at his feet, giving him thanks; and he was a Samaritan. Jesus answering said, were there not ten cleansed, but where are the nine? There are not found that returned to give glory to God, save this stranger. And he said unto him, arise, go thy way; thy faith hath made thee whole (Luke 17:11-19).

When he was come down from the mountain, great multitudes followed him and, behold, there came a leper and worshipped him, saying, Lord, if thou wilt thou canst make me clean. And Jesus put forth his hand, and touched him, saying, I will; be thou clean and immediately his leprosy was cleansed. Jesus saith unto him, see thou tell no man; but go thy way, shew thyself to the priests, and offer the gift that Moses commanded, for a testimony unto them (Matthew 8:1-4).

Analysis and Word Study

11. *through the midst of Samaria and Galilee.* Jesus was going from Ephraim (John 11:54) north through the midst of Samaria and Galilee to cross over the Jordan near Bethshean and join the Galilean group down through Perea to Jerusalem. This was the more direct route to Jerusalem.[1]

12. *there met him ten men that were lepers, which stood afar off.* The condition of lepers was characterized by an eruption of rough, scaly patches (and the erosion of toes, fingers, nose, and ears). There are other characteristics of the leper. Leprosy was a common disease of that day.[2]

They stood at a distance. The first healing of a leper (5:12-16) like this is given by Luke only.[3]

13. *lifted up their voices, and said, Jesus, Master, have mercy on us.* A failure of voice is one of the symptoms which accompany leprosy. They used what voices they had to call on Jesus.

14. *Go shew yourselves unto the priests.* With no signs of restoration upon them, they were asked to do that which implied that they were perfectly restored. Certainly, they were not being sent to the priests for healing since they did not do this. They only pronounced the person cured (Lev. 14:3,4).

As they went, they were cleansed. The men had started their journey to the priests as Jesus commanded them. They were en route.[4] Obedience to Christ brings His blessings to us.

15. *When he saw that he was healed, turned back.* One leper returned to Jesus upon realizing that he had been cured.

loud voice. Now that his voice had been fully restored, he used it to proclaim the praises of God.[5]

16. *on his face.* This shows the man's attitude of heart. He really expressed his humility and worship toward the One who had healed him.

giving him thanks: and he was a Samaritan. The very one who would have been the least expected to return and give thanks was the very one who did. The others did not feel the need to express the benefit of their healing through gratitude. The one man who felt grateful enough to return and thank Jesus for the blessing was a despised Samaritan.[6]

18. *save this stranger (Allogenes),. a foreigner. Illustrated by the inscription on the temple barrier, "let no foreigner enter within the screen and enclosure surrounding the sanctuary."*[7]

19. *Arise, go thy way; thy faith hath made thee whole.* He was still kneeling. There is a special significance to this miracle that the person who returned to thank Jesus should have been a Samaritan. The Gentiles would not be excluded from the kingdom of God but rather would receive a place in it even before those who were supposed to by birth. Faith bestowed its reward and blessing. However, he not only received the healing but also the blessing of favor from God for his thankful attitude.[8]

Interpretation and Application

Leprosy is a serious disease. It causes many terrible results in the person affected by it. First, there is a spot on the skin that begins to produce a snow-white color. The fingers would drop off one by one, thus causing the hands to become stumps. The toes of the feet were affected similarly. The face was eventually erased, as well as other parts of the body. The odor and appearance were ghastly.[9]

We need to understand the background of this dread disease. For some other diseases there was a remedy, a possible cure prescribed — but not for leprosy. It was incurable—a living death.

Leprosy was experienced in the Middle Ages. It was carried to Britain by Roman soldiers who had served in Syria in 61 B.C.

There are still many lepers in the world. It is rare in America and Britain. There are not many cases in Palestine. It still exists mostly in India, China, Malaysia, and Africa. The defeat of leprosy has been achieved mostly by using the method of isolation.

Nations did not isolate their lepers in ancient days; however, the Jews segregated themselves from the leper.

A leper was banished from society upon examination by the priest. "He shall remain unclean as long as he has the disease; he is unclean; he shall dwell alone in a habitation outside the camp" (Leviticus 13:46). The leper walked around with torn clothes, disheveled hair, a covering on his upper lip, and as he moved around he had to cry, "Unclean, unclean" (Leviticus 13:45).

Contact with a leper defiled the individual who had that contact. It was second only to the defilement caused by contact with a dead body. If a leper put his head inside a house, everything in it was considered unclean. No one was even allowed to greet a leper in an open place. A person could not stand nearer to a leper than four cubits away (a cubit is eighteen inches).[10]

It is unusual that the leper came to Jesus at all. He would never have approached an ordinary rabbi because he would have received contempt and disgust. He recognized a different quality about Jesus.

When the leper saw Jesus, he fell on his face and besought him, "Lord, if you will, you can make me clean. And He stretched out his hand, and touched him, saying, I will; be clean."[11] There was no hesitation by Jesus to heal the leper. What He had the power to do He did. An untouchable had been touched, and an unclean person had become clean. Our Lord healed the incurable and loved the unlovable.[12]

The Lord gave him a command to go to the priest and also keep quiet about his miracle. This was in accord with the customs of His day. The man did not follow the advice about keeping quiet but shared it with others.

Then we have the account of Jesus' healing ten lepers. These men had banded together and found fellowship in their condition. There is a real blessing to be realized in joining together with other people. This is the value of being an active part of the church.

These men apparently had faith that Jesus could help them even though their circumstances were seemingly beyond hope. When all else fails we still have the power of God. There is always hope because there is always God.

Jesus asserted, "All things are possible to him that believeth" (Mark 9:23). The only limit to the power of God in our lives is the limit of our belief.

Jesus instructed these men to show themselves to the priests. They had experienced no change since. They had not been healed immediately. Therefore, they could have decided it was not worth the trip. However, instead of turning away disappointed, these ten men did what He commanded. They practiced what we sing in the song, "Trust and Obey." Sometimes it requires more faith to obey than to trust.

"And it came to pass, that, as they went, they were cleansed." Life may not be easy at times, but we have to keep on living. Some people prefer death to life when the life represents pain, frustration, and misery. The children of Israel were given enough bread for each day in the wilderness. God provided for them "as they went."

Imagine what it would be like suddenly to be cured of leprosy. These men experienced it. They had suffered together, and now they were healed together. A typical human response happened after the healing. Nine of the men continued on their way, but one returned to give thanks.

We are always asking God for things. Do we remember to thank Him for the answers to prayer? Ten had asked; only one returned to praise God for his healing.[13]

True thanks is more than a courtesy. It was an expression of his heart uttered through his lips. Here was a Samaritan who had returned to give thanks from his heart. Jesus asked, "Were there not ten cleansed, but where are the nine?" Our Lord was disappointed that the others were not present as well. They, too, should have returned to praise and give thanks.

Thanksgiving should become a way of life rather than an isolated event. When it is, it is second nature to stop and thank God for each blessing that comes from Him.

We must recognize the Giver as well as the gift. In doing so, we acknowledge our need for God and that we are dependent upon Him.

The expression toward the one who gave thanks showed the feelings of Jesus: "Arise, go thy way; thy faith hath made thee whole." An expression of gratitude on our part pleases God and provides us with an even greater healing.

3
NO DISTANCE IN PRAYER
Centurion's Servant

And when Jesus was entered into Capernaum, there came unto him a centurion, beseeching him, and saying, Lord, my servant lieth at home sick of the palsy, grievously tormented. And Jesus saith unto him, I will come and heal him. The centurion answered and said, Lord, I am not worthy that thou shouldest come under my roof: but speak the word only, and my servant shall be healed. For I am a man under authority, having soldiers under me; and I say to this man, Go, and he goeth; and to another, Come, and he cometh; and to my servant, Do this, and he doeth it. When Jesus heard it, he marvelled, and said to them that followed, Verily I say unto you, I have not found so great faith, no, not in Israel. And I say unto you, that many shall come from the east and west, and shall sit down with Abraham, and Isaac, and Jacob, in the kingdom of heaven. But the children of the kingdom shall be cast out into outer darkness: there shall be weeping and gnashing of teeth. And Jesus said unto the centurion, Go thy way; and as thou has believed, so be it done unto thee. And his servant was healed in the selfsame hour (Matthew 8:5-13; also see Luke 7:1-10).

Analysis and Word Study

5. *into Capernaum.* Capernaum was a prosperous town that gained its prosperity from Tiberias. It was known for fishing activity there. Many incidents in the Gospels relate to this town. Here was the household of Peter; here there were healings recorded such as the paralytic; and here was the home of that believing court official, whose child Jesus had healed.

a centurion. The centurion was one who had learned to love Israel and reverence Israel's God, one who had built a synagogue for the Jews.

6. *grievously tormented.* The boy (servant) was a bedridden paralytic.

7. *I will come and heal him.* The word for heal here means to give medical attention, then restore to health. Jesus is like a physician who takes care of (cures) the sick. He is the Great Physician who has all power to meet each person's need.[2]

8. *speak the word only.* The centurion recognized the power of the word from Christ. It would be sufficient.

9. *For I am a man under authority, having soldiers under me.* He had learned obedience to his superiors and therefore expected obedience to his commands, instant obedience. He recognized the authority of Jesus over illness.

10. *so great faith.* Though found in a Roman centurion, it was even greater than that of any Jew.

11. *sit down.* Recline at table on couches as Jews and Romans did.

12. *children of the kingdom shall be cast out into outer darkness: shall be weeping and gnashing of teeth.* The Jews believed that they had a special right to the kingdom because they were descendants of Abraham (Matt. 3:9). However, natural birth did not guarantee them a place in the kingdom. Just the opposite: they would be put in the darkness that exists outside the limits of the lighted palace, one of the figures for hell or punishment (Matt. 23:13, 25:30).[3]

13. *as thou hast believed...servant was healed in the selfsame hour.* Again, faith results in healing and blessing.

Interpretation and Application

When Jesus arrived at Capernaum, He was approached by the elders on behalf of a centurion whose servant was sick. This centurion was a friend of the Jews and had built them a synagogue. Jesus immediately responded to the request by traveling to the centurion's house. However, on the way He was met by friends with a message from the centurion. The centurion felt unworthy for Jesus to visit his house. All He had to do was simply speak the word, and his servant would be healed. The centurion was familiar with giving orders and seeing them obeyed. He believed that Jesus could merely speak the word, and his servant would be healed. When Jesus heard this He stated that nowhere in Israel had He found such faith. When the friends returned, they found the servant well.

A centurion incident makes an interesting study. A Roman legion consisted of 6,000 men and was divided into sixty centuries, each under the direction of a centurion. The centurions were the backbone of the Roman army. They signed up for twenty years and were the commanding strength of the army. The most honored of all was the one who was given "command of the eagle," which was the standard of the legion.[4]

There are other centurions mentioned in the New Testament. There was the centurion who spoke of Jesus as the Son of God while Jesus was on the cross. Cornelius was the first Gentile convert of the church; there was the centurion who discovered that Paul was a Roman citizen and provided him protection: there was the centurion who was told of a plot to kill Paul and moved into action to stop it; there was the centurion who looked after Paul, which was an order from Felix; there was the centurion who was with Paul on the trip to Rome and treated him courteously.

This centurion from Capernaum was most likely a Gentile. The law provided that a Jew was not supposed to enter a Gentile's house. The centurion was probably following this law.

The Romans had a kind of military service that was compulsory, but the Jews were exempt from it. They were exempt because the law forbade them from carrying arms on the sabbath day because to do so would mean carrying a burden.[5]

There is an interesting relationship between the master and the servant. The servant was always subject to the will of the master. They could be and often were treated cruelly.

A writer named Petrus wrote that: "Whatever a master does to a slave, undeservedly, in anger, willingly, unwillingly, in forgetfulness, after careful thought, knowingly, unknowingly, is judgment, justice and law."[6]

However, the centurion of this event in the Scriptures must have cared tremendously for his servant—a tremendous testimony for a true man of faith.

It is marvelous that the centurion could believe for a miracle at a distance. He did not think it was necessary for Jesus to touch or lay hands on his servant, or even be present physically.

There are certain interesting experiences that relate to knowledge and fact being received at a distance. When a man named Swedenborg was in Gotenborg in 1759, he described a fire occurring in Stockholm 300 miles away. His account of the fire to the authorities named the owner of the house that was burned and reported when the fire was put out.

A French experimenter, Dr. Janet, was able to hypnotize certain people at a distance. Dr. Janet was successful in putting the person into a trance at the time attempted in eighteen out of twenty-five attempts.[7]

James promised, "The prayer of faith shall save the sick" (James 5:15). The faith here was in the person doing the praying. Praying for other people can cause astounding results.

Charles L. Allen, the great writer and preacher, related how he prayed for people who requested it. He sought to have a clear mental picture of the person. Then he imaged a picture in his mind of Christ. He then sought to bring the two together. Since the person requesting prayer may not have had as much faith as would have been desired, he substituted his own faith and brought the individual into contact with it for the need to be met.[8]

Jesus was amazed at the centurion's faith. We can also arrive at this kind of faith in several ways. Here are a few suggestions.

To begin with, we need to be more aware of Jesus Christ. This involves knowing Him personally. It also includes a knowledge of His life on earth. This means careful readings of the Gospels. Second, the centurion supported the church. He was interested in the work of God and helped support it. Actively supporting the church strengthens our faith. Third, the centurion had humility. "I am not worthy that thou shouldest enter under my roof." A person with pride does not recognize his need of God. Fourth, the centurion showed concern for others. He was not selfish but reached out in faith to others in need. He wanted to see his servant healed and well. Fifth, the centurion recognized the authority and power of God. This is a giant step to believing faith under all circumstances. Truly, there is no distance in prayer.

4

THE TOUCH OF FAITH
Woman Afflicted for Twelve Years

And a certain woman, which had an issue of blood twelve years, and had suffered many things of many physicians, and had spent all that she had, and was nothing better, but rather grew worse, when she had heard of Jesus, came in the press behind, and touched his garment. For she said, if I may touch but his clothes, I shall be whole. And straightway the fountain of her blood was dried up; and she felt in her body that she was healed of that plague. and Jesus, immediately knowing in himself that virtue had gone out of him, turned him about in the press, and said, Who touched my clothes? And his disciples said unto him, Thou seest the multitude thronging thee, and sayest thou, Who touched me? And he looked round about to see her that had done this thing. But the woman fearing and trembling, knowing what was done in her, came and fell down before him, and told him all the truth. And he said unto her, Daughter, thy faith hath made thee whole; go in peace, and be whole of thy plague (Mark 5:25-34; also Matthew 9:20-22; Luke 8:43-48).

Analysis and Word Study

25,26. *had suffered many things of many physicians.* This is a pathetic picture of a woman with a chronic case who had tried many doctors. The meaning here is "to suffer pain." It does not refer only to subjection to treatment.

had spent all that she had ... grew worse. All her treatment did not aid her or cure her. It had taken all her resources.[1]

21

27,28. *When she had heard of Jesus.* The literal meaning is "having heard of the things concerning the Jesus." The English name "Jesus" is the transliteration of the Hebrew name "Jehoshua." The name "Joshua" was a common name in Palestine, and the definite article is used by the Gospel writers often to distinguish our Lord from others of the same name.[2]

in the press. This means the crowd.

touched his garment...If I may touch but his clothes, I shall be whole. She did not want to attract attention. She possibly was shy or timid. She crept up in the crowd and touched the hem or border of his garment. (*kraspedon*) according to Matthew 9:20 and Luke 8:44.[3]

29. *She felt in her body.* She knew that she was healed. It was a genuine moment of joy for her. The plague (*mastigos*) or scourge was a whip used in flagellations as on Paul to find out his guilt (Acts 22:24; Heb. 11:36).

30. *knowing in himself.* Jesus perceived in himself that power had gone out from him. Here Jesus seems to say: "I felt in Myself the power from Me go."

Who touched my clothes? More precisely, it was, "Who touched me on my clothes?" It was a dramatic moment for Jesus and this woman. It became a regular practice for people to touch the hem of the garment of Jesus and be healed (Mark 6:56).[4]

31. *Thronging thee.* There were many people around Jesus when the woman touched Him. Jesus had the utmost sympathy. It was a drain on His energy to heal so many people.

32. *And he looked round about.* He kept looking around to find out. Jesus could tell the difference between the touch of the crowd and the touch of the woman.

33. *Fearing and trembling, knowing.* She had heard the question from Jesus and felt His gaze. She knew she must confess what had happened. Secrecy was no longer possible.[5]

34. *And he said to her, Daughter.* She would receive the sympathy that Christ offered expressed in this word: *Thugater*, daughter, to a mature woman. He is speaking here as a father to a child.

Go in peace. The peace that relates to body and soul that comes from the Hebrew word *shalom.*

Be whole of thy plague. Be continually whole. The latter word is the translation of *hugies,* "to be sound of body," from which we get our word "hygienic." "Plague" is *mastix,* "a whip, plague, a calamity or misfortune," used of distressing bodily diseases.[6]

Interpretation and Application

Jesus was going to the house of Jairus, the ruler of the synagogue, whose daughter was sick. There was a woman in the crowd who had suffered from an incurable problem.

The trouble she was having was common in Palestine. There were many kinds of remedies and treatments recommended for it. She had tried everything, had gone to many physicians, but instead of becoming better, she grew worse.

This kind of illness made her unclean. The law stated that she could not attend the synagogue service. She was separated from all religious and social life.[7]

She had been sick for twelve years when she came behind Jesus and touched the hem of His garment. The hem was simply the fringe. A tassel was tied to each of the four corners of the outer garment. There was a cloak that was used for clothing by day and as a blanket at night. The loose end of the cloak probably was hung over Jesus' left shoulder, and the tassel attached to it could have been touched by someone who came up behind him.[8]

It is important to realize she was not the only person touching Him. In fact, there were so many people around Jesus that the apostles were amazed when He spoke of being touched by someone. There was obviously a large crowd of people present. However, Jesus turned all of His attention to this woman. She was the main one that mattered at that moment. She was a part of the crowd, but Jesus stopped when she touched Him. The individual has always been important to Jesus. Augustine expressed it long ago: "God loves each one of us as if there were only one of us to love."

Another fact concerning this healing is that it drained energy from Jesus. He remarked that power had gone out of Him. A Dr. Racanelli of Florence relates some interesting experiences with his handling of people. He practices the laying on of hands for people who are sick. He states that while the patient is left with a sense of well-being, he himself experiences a tremendous amount of fatigue and has to be careful not to become exhausted.[9]

It was not enough that the woman had been healed. Jesus wanted to know who had touched Him with such faith. He used the term "daughter." This signified a tender compassion for the woman. "Your faith has made you well." He wanted to bring her face to face with Himself.[10]

Jesus was the only person in twelve years who met her need. This is the sublime truth that reaches to our day. Are you having difficulties in your marriage? Is there a problem in your family? Are you having trouble in your job? Are you depressed, lonely, and frustrated about your circumstances? Does life seem to be grabbing more from you than you can stand? Are your finances creating difficulty and debt? Well, God has a miracle for each person. There is hope for you.

Have you ever asked yourself the question, "What is a miracle?" *Webster's Dictionary* defines it as "an event or action that apparently contradicts known scientific laws and is hence thought to be due to supernatural causes, especially an act of God."[11]

Remember, there was no power in the clothes of Jesus to heal this woman. She touched Jesus with her faith. The hem of his garment was only a point of contact for her healing. However, it was a contact to be cured. She really believed that when she touched the "hem of His garment" she would be cured. I contend she could have touched any part of His clothes and received the same healing power. What about your need today? I have heard of people using various means to reach out in faith. Some of them have touched their television, believed, and received. Others have believed when they received the bread and cup in the Lord's Supper. Their need would not be met, and yet it was. It is not the object of your touch that is important but rather *the person of Christ*. He represents healing and deliverance.

Out of the thronging multitude only one touched the hem with the "hand" of faith. There were obviously many other people who needed healing that day, but they did not have the faith of this woman.

Also, there are many people today who are having outward contact with Christ through His church. However, they are not really in touch with the Son of God. They are in touch with what he represents but not actually in touch with Him personally.[12]

It requires a personal touch to reach God—a touch of faith to receive from God.

Are you reaching? Are you touching? Are you believing? Are you receiving? He is alive, ready, and waiting. Reach out and touch Jesus today with your faith.

Remember, the touch of faith receives its miracle.

5
HEALING AT HOME
Peter's Mother-in-Law

*And when Jesus was come into Peter's house, he saw his
wife's mother laid, and sick of a fever. And he touched her
hand, and the fever left her: and she arose, and ministered
unto them. (Matthew 8:14,15) (Also Mark 1:29-31; Luke
4:38,39).*

Analysis and Word Study

14. *Peter's house.* Peter was married, and Andrew and Peter's
mother-in-law lived with him. Jesus always stayed at Peter's house
when He was in Capernaum.[1]

Wife's mother laid, and sick of a fever. (*biblemenen kai peres-
sousan*). She had a burning with fever. This speaks of continuous
action or a state in past time. She had been sick for a period of time.
We are not sure exactly how long. "Of a fever," *puresso*, "to be sick
with a fever" are the words used. The noun form is the Greek word
for fire. "Stretched out with a fever." Luke uses the medical term,
"holden with a great fever." Luke speaks of Jesus standing over her
like a doctor.[2]

15. *Touched her hand.* Like any good doctor would do, he
touched her hand. Also, He did it in loving sympathy as the Great
Physician.[3] The touch of God brought healing to her body.

Ministered unto them. "Began to minister" (*diekonei*). The cure
must have been instantaneous, to make it possible for Peter's mother-
in-law to cook a meal for Jesus and His men. She felt gratitude and
love at being healed.[4]

27

Interpretation and Application

Jesus' accommodations for living were simple. He occasionally stayed with people in their homes. There is no record of all His private activities. It seems that He and His disciples "roughed it" through life. The life of Christ in the New Testament was a transient one, not domestic. We see Jesus walking on the water, on the shore, sleeping and praying outside under the stars at night. Here we find Him visiting in the home of Simon and Andrew. He was a house guest in the home of Mary and Martha. Jesus was constantly among people, except for the time He spent apart in prayer.

He was with Peter, James, and John, along with other followers. They had been together in the synagogue service as was their custom. Jesus had only recently missed being murdered in Nazareth. He had been reading His favorite Scripture from Isaiah about His being anointed ... "to preach the gospel to the poor ... heal the broken-hearted ... " Everything went well until He mentioned Naaman the Syrian being the only leper cleansed in the time of the prophet Elisha. Then they became enraged and sought to kill Him, but He escaped.

Another time "he went down to Capernaum ... and he was teaching them on the sabbath ... " An insane person made known his possession by devils and Jesus healed him. It seems that the hometown of Simon treated Jesus well.[5]

The Jewish day began at 6 A.M. Jesus and His companions had gone to Peter's house after the synagogue service. Jesus had just completed His works in the synagogue, but He was never too tired to help and heal.

Peter's mother-in-law was suffering from "a burning fever," which was a most prevalent sickness in that part of Galilee. The Talmud explains how they dealt with it. A knife made of iron was tied by some hair to a thorn bush. Some verses from Exodus were repeated on certain days. A magical formula was given, and the cure was supposedly achieved.

Jesus disregarded all of the above and simply with a gesture and a word of authority and power, healed her. The word used for authority in the passage is *exousia*; and *exousia* was defined as unique knowledge coupled with unique power. This is what Jesus possessed and what He exercised in the house. Paul Tournier, a

28

Christian doctor, wrote, "My patients often say to me, 'I admire the patience with which you listen to everything I tell you.' It is not patience at all, but interest." A miracle to Jesus was not something done to increase His prestige. He healed instinctively, because He was extremely interested in everyone who needed His help.[6]

It is intriguing to note that the three accounts give three ideas about what Jesus did. One reports that Jesus stood over her; another, He touched her hand; the third, He lifted her up. They all agree that the fever left her.

We realize that pain, sickness, delirium, and madness, are as much infringements of the laws of nature as the miracles themselves. They do not represent the normal existence for humanity but rather the opposite of what God intends for us. It is imperative that we recognize our intense need for God, not only in the sunshine of health but also in the cloud of suffering.

Pain is an ugly, unlovely, and terrible reality. No one wants to experience it. This is realized quickly when a visit to the doctor requires a simple shot in the arm. Even that becomes an unpleasant happening. It is obvious that Jesus disliked pain. This means that God dislikes it.[7] Some people have the mistaken idea that God somehow adds constant pain and discomfort to their lives to make them conform more perfectly to His will. One only needs to remember that Jesus healed even those whose lives were not as right or righteous as they should be. True, God does allow many bad circumstances in our lives but turns them around to our good. Peter's mother-in-law had a raging fever. She was tossing from side to side. Her head ached, her senses were confused, and she felt terrible.

All of a sudden everything changed. A cooling breath wiped away the burning heat of the fever; a clearness of mind replaced the confusion of her thoughts; there was a realization of light where there had been darkness; a calmness occurred instead of restlessness. What a blessing to experience the Master's ministry.

It was first seen upon the hay.
It was found next upon a cheek.
Time passed and it grew stronger each year,
until the hammer it held yielded beneath each blow.

A fevered brow quickly became cool.
A crippled limb made to walk.
The troubled mind now calm and serene.
The blind eye caused to see.
Children did not escape its touch.
A miracle lies within its reach.
Twenty centuries long, it stretches forth still,
To meet our needs,

His healing hand.

The disciples had learned by now to present their needs to Jesus. It was second nature to share this need with Him. The hymn expresses it aptly, "Take your burden to the Lord and leave it there." The disciples of Jesus had learned a spiritual practice that became a habit for a lifetime—to share all their worries and cares with Jesus and to ask His help for them. We need to do the same because Jesus still cares about our every need.

There is another truth in this passage of Scripture that we must not miss. Peter's wife's mother began to care for their needs as soon as she was healed. She used her regained health for renewed service.[8]

Health is sustained in the avenue of service. Spiritual and physical health cannot be achieved totally independent of God. It is even recorded of those in heaven that "They serve him day and night."

There is strength in service, and there should be service when there is strength. A healthy body should fulfil the responsibility of helping others.

We should not despise the commonplace areas of service. Sometimes we seek for a "great work" to do while there is ample opportunity for work right at hand.[9]

6
WINDS AND WATER
Sea Calmed

And when he was entered into a ship, his disciples followed him. And, behold, there arose a great tempest in the sea, insomuch that the ship was covered with the waves: but he was asleep. And his disciples came to him, and awoke him, saying, Lord, save us: we perish. And he saith unto them, Why are ye fearful, O ye of little faith? Then he arose, and rebuked the winds and the sea; and there was a great calm. But the men marvelled, saying, What manner of man is this, that even the winds and the sea obey him! (Matthew 8:23-27; also Mark 4:35-41; Luke 8:22-25).

Analysis and Word Study

24. *Tempest.* (*Seismos*) a shaking.[1]

But He was asleep. (*autos de ekatheunden*)— "was sleeping." The Sea of Galilee is 680 feet below the Mediterranean Sea. There are times when sudden squalls come down from the summit of Hermon with terrific force (*seismos megas*) like an earthquake. Mark (4:37) and Luke (8:23) call it a whirlwind (*lailaps*) in furious gusts.[2]

25. *Save us: we perish.* The more precise meaning would be, "Lord, save us at once because we are perishing." They were fearful.

26. *O ye of little faith.* Jesus spoke to rebuke them for not using the faith they had. They did not even apply the faith. He was upset because of their excess of terror which they displayed. There was so little understanding in their minds and lives that they would be so afraid with Jesus on board or in the ship.[3]

Rebuked. Jesus came against all forces that would destroy. He represents life and harmony. He rebuked the winds just as elsewhere He rebuked a fever (Luke 4:39).[4]

27. *Even the winds and the sea obey Him.* A nature miracle. Even a sudden drop in the wind would not calm the sea immediately.[5]

Interpretation and Application

The miracle related was vividly impressed upon me when I was in Birmingham, Alabama, on a trip. I was staying at a motel downtown when the television newscaster announced that a tornado was sighted heading directly toward us. I thought about the experience of Jesus and His men in the boat. I hurried to my room and asked God to keep the tornado away from us. Then I sought to comfort myself by remembering how Jesus had consoled them not to be afraid. The tornado did some damage, but its direction changed.

This miracle is important because we have many occasions when fear virtually paralyzes.

Jesus had been preaching in Galilee, on the Western side of the Sea of Galilee. The evening was approaching, and there were many people surrounding Jesus. He requested His disciples to row Him across to the other side of the lake. They started out in the boat, along with some other smaller boats. The Lake of Gennesaret was liable to sudden and severe storms. Wind would rush down through the mountains and in a moment the water would become violent.[6] It was such a storm that descended on the group as they crossed the sea because "the boat was covered with the waves." It must have been a severe storm for experienced fishermen familiar with the lake to become frightened.

Jesus was tired when the journey began and had fallen asleep in the stern of the boat. Neither the strong wind nor the violent sea caused Him to wake up.

The disciples decided to awaken the Lord with words of urgency because they feared for their lives. It would seem, from a comparison of the three accounts of Matthew, Mark, and Luke, that our Lord first gently rebuked the disciples for their fear before He calmed the wind and sea. Then, He again spoke to His disciples, asking "Where is your faith?" The calming of the sea was a total experience in that the water became smooth and unruffled.

God always put harmony back into the things or persons that have been disrupted. In this case, nature had been disrupted and was a threat to their well-being. Whether it was a storm on the sea or a storm of sickness or demon possession, Jesus restored and brought harmony. We can look forward to a final and lasting harmony through the rule of God.[7]

The wind and the sea obeyed Christ. There was an immediate response to His command. Even a sudden drop in the wind would not at once calm the sea.[8]

We must remember that Jesus rebuked the wind. He also rebuked the fever, and He rebuked the demons. It is obvious that He is against the forces which would hurt or destroy us. We can trust Christ always to do right by us. We need to call on Him more often for our lives to become straight spiritually, for our fears to be calmed, and for our needs to be met. The sea is a symbol of the restless and sinful world.[9] We need to call on God to help bring about the miracles called for in our world today.

Whether or not we admit it, fear affects each of us. It can assume many forms. Some are afraid of life, others of sickness, of the future, of death, of misfortune. Many are afraid of one another. A forced smile and a quick burst of laughter conceal and reveal this fact. There is fear of failure, fear of environmental hazards, fear of nuclear war, fear of tomorrow. Fear causes frustration; frustration creates depression; and depression may lead to suicide. Many feel as if they are sinking and about to perish.

Why are we so fearful? Many answers can be given, but the main one is our lack of faith in God. The most potent antidote to fear is not courage, but faith. Without God we are bound to be afraid. We cannot live without the hope and trust that God provides.

Kagawa, a Japanese leader, was bombarded by fear, but he was led to Christ, and through Him found help. He read and reread the Scriptures about how God clothes the lilies and feeds the birds. He realized God would provide for him, and his fear vanished.[10]

This, however, presents a problem. How is it that there are people who profess to know God personally and who live in His love and care, and yet are often anxious and afraid? We are souls living in bodies, and each person is an individual personality. If a person has been reared in an atmosphere of tension, nervousness, and anxiety, they will probably be tense, nervous, and anxious.

Now, simply to tell this person to be calm is not enough to calm him. His whole character is programmed for fear instead of faith. One of the primary reasons we do not witness more often to others about Jesus is fear, fear of failure, fear of what the person will think or say or do. Why don't people merely witness in faith and not worry about these things? They would if they had been trained to do so. When they have experienced "witnessing" often enough, they lose the fear. Many people could benefit from an entire course on faith.

The disciples spent three years at the side of Christ and yet were immobilized by fear when Jesus died on the cross.

In order to have a fear-conquering faith, we must stay daily in the school of Christ's teaching and in the classroom of His presence. He always teaches us to believe, to have faith. He never instructs us to fear and be afraid. Most of our fears are based on circumstances. We must realize that Christ is in control of circumstances when we call on Him. First, we need to ask for help. Second, we need to believe He will help. Third, we need to trust Him in the middle of whatever happens.

7

FULL OF DEVILS
The Man with an Unclean Spirit

And they came over unto the other side of the sea, into the country of the Gadarenes. And when he was come out of the ship, immediately there met him out of the tombs a man with an unclean spirit, Who had his dwelling among the tombs; and no man could bind him, no, not with chains: Because that he had been often bound with fetters and chains, and the chains had been plucked asunder by him, and the fetters broken in pieces: neither could any man tame him. And always, night and day, he was in the mountains, and in the tombs, crying, and cutting himself with stones. But when he saw Jesus afar off, he ran and worshipped him, And cried with a loud voice, and said, What have I to do with thee, Jesus, thou Son of the most high God? I adjure thee by God, that thou torment me not. For he said unto him, Come out of the man, thou unclean spirit. And he asked him, What is thy name? And he answered, saying, My name is Legion: for we are many. And he besought him much that he would not send them away out of the country. Now there was there nigh unto the mountains a great herd of swine feeding. And all the devils besought him, saying, Send us into the swine, that we may enter into them. And forthwith Jesus gave them leave. And the unclean spirits went out, and entered into the swine: and the herd ran violently down a steep place into the sea, (they were about two thousand;) and were choked in the sea. And they that fed the swine fled, and told it in the city, and in the country. And they went out to see what it was that was done. And they come to Jesus, and see him that was possessed with the devil, and had the legion, sitting, and clothed, and in his right mind: and they were afraid. And they that saw it told them how it befell to him that was possessed with the devil, and also concerning the swine. And they began to pray him to depart out of their coasts. And when he was come into the ship, he that had been possessed with the devil prayed him that he might be with him. Howbeit Jesus suffered him not, but saith unto him, Go home to thy friends, and tell them how great things the Lord hath done for thee, and hath had compassion on thee (Mark 5:1-19; also Matthew 8:28-34; Luke 8:26-39).

Analysis and Word Study

1. *Gadarenes.* The ruins of the village Khersa (Gerasa) probably point to this site which is in the district of Gadara some six miles southeastward, not to the city of Gerasa thirty miles away.

2. *Out of the ship ... a man with an unclean spirit.* The demoniac greeted Jesus at once. Each Gospel contains a different phrase. Mark has "a man with an unclean spirit" (*en pheumati akathartoi*), Matthew 8:28— "two possessed with demons" (*duo daimonizomenoi*), Luke 8:17— "one having demons" (*tis echon daimonia*).[1]

3. *Who had his dwelling among the tombs.* The idea here represents a settled habitation, a place away from the cities, a remote place that would attract those who sought to flee from the fellowship of others.

4. *Bound with fetters and chains.* "Fetters" is the translation of *pede*, a fetter or shackle for the feet. The word comes from *peza*— "the foot or instep." The demonized man was bound both by his hands and his feet. He was strong enough to sever the chains and the fetters. "Tame" is *damazo*, "to restrain, curb, tame."[2]

5. *Crying, and cutting himself with stones.* Night and day his loud scream could be heard. The verb for cutting himself means to cut down. He was probably full of scars and gashes all over his body.

6. *Ran and worshipped.* It was quite an experience for the disciples to see this man wild and naked suddenly turn to worship.

7. *I adjure thee by God.* He calls Jesus here "Son of the Most High God," as in Luke 8:28.

36

8. *Torment me not.* The word means to test metals and then to test one by torture.[3]

9. *My name is Legion.* A full Roman legion had 6,826 men.

13. *And Jesus gave them leave.* He gave them permission to enter the swine. It was better for hogs to perish than men, but the loss of property raises a difficulty of its own.

They were choked (*apnigonto*). This is in the imperfect tense, picturing the disappearance of pig after pig in the sea.[4]

14. *They that fed the swine fled.* The implication is clear that the swineherds were afraid because of the destruction of the hogs and ran away.

15. *They see him that was possessed with the devil.* This word (see) used here is *theoreo* and speaks of a critical, searching investigation.

In his right mind. A return to sanity and self-control.

16. *Told them.* Gave a complete report of what had happened.[5]

17. *To depart out of their coasts.* The people of Nazareth had driven Jesus away (Luke 4:16-31). The owners of the hogs cared more for the loss of their property than for the healing of the demoniac.

19. *Go home to thy friends.* The people who needed the message about Jesus were those who were asking Him to leave. Jesus wanted this man to witness to those who knew him.[6]

Interpretation and Application

Jesus performed this miracle on the other side of the Sea of Galilee in the area of Decapolis. Decapolis means, in the literal sense, "The Ten Cities." These were beautiful cities; they had their temples, their theatres, and their gods. This is the first reference to the gospel going to the Gentile world.

The miracle occurred in an awfully grim place. There were many caves in that location, and those particular caves were used as tombs. It was a proper place for a demon-possessed person to live. No sane person would come near the site.

Jesus and His disciples had crossed the Sea of Galilee. It is possible that they arrived at night.[7] The man was a demoniac because the Scripture states he was full of demons. Our Lord referred to demons as "evil spirits," not merely evil influences but evil agents of Satan, those who were under the direction and control of the prince of demons. They were "commanded" to come out. They "testified," from their own supernatural knowledge, that Jesus was the "Son of God Most High!" They "prayed" Him not to send them "into the deep," the bottomless pit, their original home. They "asked permission" to enter a herd of swine. In obedience to Christ's word they "departed" out of their victim and further manifested their personality by "entering into" the herd of swine and thus causing the whole herd to race off of a steep cliff into the sea. Jesus addressed the demons dwelling in the man as distinct personal agents.

"Demoniac" is the name whereby antiquity designated sufferers from mental diseases. It was held that the mentally deranged, lunatics, epileptics, and the hysterical were possessed by evil spirits. Modern explanations of these conditions do not eliminate the fact that in many cases the demoniac is such in the truest sense of the word.[8]

The explanation for mental disorders, accepted both by the learned and by the common people, served Jesus well in the form of teaching He adopted. It was the mission of Christ to build the kingdom of God and overthrow that of Satan. To cast out demons, therefore, was part of His mission. He was not concerned to distinguish between disorders due to sin and those due to possession by evil spirits. There exists a parallelism between bodily and spiritual ills which language itself has consecrated and which is based upon a true affinity. The madman and the epileptic, the slothful man and the paralytic, he who is impure and the leper, the blind man and he who cannot see truth, he who is dead and he who will not listen to truth, he who is saved and he who is resurrected.[9]

It is often difficult for us to believe in what we cannot see. If we could see a demon, we would immediately become a believer.

We can discover some interesting characteristics of Jesus concerning this miracle. *First, Jesus had no fear in dealing with such a case.* It would be a dangerous dare even to approach a violent maniac like this man, but Jesus did it with supreme courage.

Sir James Simpson tried chloroform, first on himself and his colleagues. Simpson and two medical colleagues filled tumblers with chloroform. They experienced all of the sensations of its effects and went to sleep for a time. They risked their lives to save others from pain.[10]

Jesus was safe in dealing with this man in the same manner. He was always safe. He was and is the Son of God and had ultimate power and control over any and all circumstances.

Second, Jesus did not show superiority. He showed His usual compassion and kindness toward this man whom He cured. There are times when Christians act superior to others. They become inflated with their own self-righteousness, and that hinders their effectiveness for God. We need to be aware of the kind of concern and compassion that Jesus had and to practice it ourselves.

Third, Jesus did not show repulsion. No one else in Decapolis would have approached this madman. Jesus is the perfect example for every person who has sought to bring healing and help to those who are in sin, or who are suffering from some physical or mental illness.

Here we find Heaven's greatest ambassador meeting hell's greatest representative. And yet, the man came before Jesus with an attitude of worship. The demons well recognized who Jesus was. They requested that He not torment them.

The first effort of Christ to exorcise the demons did not result in obedience. They did not abandon the man immediately. Rather, we have a dialogue of desire on the part of the unclean spirits. They did not want to be sent "out of the country" or into "the deep." Both statements represent the same truth because, according to Jewish ideas, being sent out of their own country implied being sent into the abyss or "bottomless pit."[11] Instead, they requested to be sent into the herd of swine. Jesus gave them permission to do this. It resulted in the destruction of the swine. This is a typical result of the power of Satan. He stands for destruction. "The thief cometh not, but for to steal, and to kill, and to destroy: I am come that they might have life, and that they might have it more abundantly" (John 10:10). This verse is carried out through this miracle. The demons were in the process of destroying this man but Jesus came to deliver him and give him a sane and serene mind.

39

8
A MEAL FOR THE MULTITUDES
Five Thousand Fed

After these things Jesus went over the sea of Galilee, which is the sea of Tiberias. And a great multitude followed him, because they saw his miracles which he did on them that were diseased. And Jesus went up into a mountain, and there he sat with his disciples. And the passover, a feast of the Jews, was nigh. When Jesus then lifted up his eyes, and saw a great company come unto him, he saith unto Philip, Whence shall we buy bread, that these may eat? And this he said to prove him: for he himself knew what he would do. Philip answered him, Two hundred pennyworth of bread is not sufficient for them, that every one of them may take a little. One of his disciples, Andrew, Simon Peter's brother, saith unto him, There is a lad here, which hath five barley loaves, and two small fishes: but what are they among so many? And Jesus said, Make the men sit down. Now there was much grass in the place. So the men sat down, in number about five thousand. And Jesus took the loaves; and when he had given thanks, he distributed to the disciples, and the disciples to them that were set down; and likewise of the fishes as much as they would. When they were filled, he said unto his disciples, Gather up the fragments that remain, that nothing be lost. Therefore they gathered them together, and filled twelve baskets with the fragments of the five barley loaves, which remained over and above unto them that had eaten (John 6:1-13; also Matthew 14:13-21; Mark 6:30-44; Luke 9:10-17).

Analysis and Word Study

1. *After these things.* This does not relate to an immediate sequence of events. A much longer period of time — a whole year is a possibility.[1]

2. *Followed.* (*edolouthei*). A crowd of people who wished to receive the benefit of His healing power mobbed Him.

3. *Into a mountain.* Mark (6:46) and Matthew (14:23) mention that after the miracle Jesus went farther up into the mountain to pray.

4. *A feast of the Jews.* This is probably the third Passover in the ministry of Jesus. Jesus did not attend this Passover because of the hostility in Jerusalem (7:1).[2]

7. *Pennyworth of bread.* Two hundred pennyworth would represent between thirty and thirty-five dollars.

9. *Five barley loaves, and two small fishes.* The word (barley) occurs here and in verse 13 in the New Testament. It seemed to be an inferior type of bread not considered very high in food quality. The fish were eaten with the bread.

10. *Sit down.* They reclined on the grass in different groups of people.[3]

11. *When He had given thanks.* Jesus prayed before He ate a meal. It was the usual grace before meals here.

12. *And when they were filled.* The people were all satisfied. Then, they began to gather up the pieces left over.

13. *Twelve baskets.* (*dodeka kophinous*). It is thought there was one for each of the apostles. These were stout wicker baskets in contrast to the soft type used at the feeding of the four thousand. Here all the Gospels (Mark 6:43; Matt. 14:20; Luke 9:17; John 6:13) use *kophinoi*. The same distinction between *kophinoi* and *sphwides* is preserved in the allusion to the incidents by Jesus in Mark 8:19 and 20 and Matthew 16:9 and 10.[4]

Interpretation and Application

There are more than thirty miracles of Jesus recorded in one or more of the four Gospels, *but only one of those miracles is recorded by all four of the Gospel writers.* That miracle is the feeding of the five thousand.

Here is the account. Jesus and His disciples were tired and sought to withdraw by themselves for a rest. They were surrounded by people constantly. This happens to many of us today. We are so busy we do not take time to rest properly. Neither do we take enough time to be with God. Many do not observe Sunday correctly. No wonder there is so much nervous tension today. Many have called this the "age of anxiety."

James Browne, a famous physician, wrote: "We doctors, in the treatment of nervous diseases, are now constantly compelled to prescribe periods of rest. Such periods are, I think, only Sundays in arrears."[5]

This generation needs to learn how to relax better. Like the old woman who commented, "I have learned to sit loose," we need to remember that if we never learn to let go, there may come a time when we will not be able to hang on. "Come ye yourselves apart into a desert place, and rest awhile," Jesus invited.

As they tried to retreat, however, the people followed them. The word quickly spread, and soon a crowd of five thousand men, probably not counting women and children, had gathered. The Bible reveals that Jesus was "moved with compassion" when He saw them. He beheld their needs and wanted to help them. The multitudes wanted to be near Christ because they knew He had the power to effect mighty miracles. He loved the people, and they responded to His love. He would preach, teach, and heal them. The time, though, had come for them to eat. They were hungry, and Jesus was receptive to meeting this need as well. Our Lord who taught us to pray, "Give us this day our daily bread," was willing to use His miraculous power to provide for the physical needs of the people.[6]

Some people think that God is only interested in the spiritual aspects of our lives, but He is also concerned about our need for food, clothes, and other necessities of life. We should pray about our church. We should carry our financial needs to the Lord in prayer even as we beseech Him for our spiritual needs.

The disciples could think only of sending the multitudes away to secure their own food. They were seeking to be relieved of any responsibility for the people. Sometimes, we attempt the same—we want to flee our responsibilities. Some people even commit suicide because they cannot cope with the pressures of responsibility placed on them.

Another tendency people have is to procrastinate. We lean toward putting off tasks until a later time.

Again, the disciples failed to realize who was with them. They bypassed considering the power of God.

Jesus did not want to send away people who needed to be sustained physically. God always has a plan to provide for every situation. Nothing ever takes God by surprise. We are constantly worried about a thousand and one things relating to the present and the future, but God has everything under control. He has a plan for each one of us, and He has a plan for our nation and our world. He will never be defeated.

Christ asked the defeated disciples, "How many loaves have you?" Andrew replied, probably hesitantly, "There is a lad here with five barley loaves and two small fish, but what are they among so many?" How many times do we react in this manner to our circumstances and inadequate resources? We tend so often to act as if God is impersonal and far removed.

Here is a touching picture of a boy who gave all of his food to Jesus. He must have been hungry, too. He also must have trusted the Lord. It is sad when a person seeks to keep what belongs to God. Their time, talents, and tithes—their lives themselves—belong to God.

Jesus gave thanks. Charles Allen suggests four pictures he would like to see painted on canvas. One would be of the young boy giving his food to Jesus. Another would show Christ at a table with His disciples where "He took bread, and gave thanks" (Luke 22:19).

The third picture depicts a ship in the midst of a raging storm at sea. There were 276 people on board. For fourteen days they had been blown by the storm, and they were afraid. Then Paul stood up and before all of them "took bread and gave thanks to God" (Acts 27:35). The fourth portrait portrays a small group of people who had only a year before come to America, a new land. They faced many hardships, but they knelt to thank God for their blessings.[7]

44

Gratefully accept the resources you have and, with God's help, they will prove sufficient.

9
WALKING ON WATER
Jesus Walking on the Sea

And straightway Jesus constrained his disciples to get into a ship, and to go before him unto the other side, while he sent the multitudes away. And when he had sent the multitudes away, he went up into a mountain apart to pray: and when the evening was come, he was there alone. But the ship was now in the midst of the sea, tossed with waves: for the wind was contrary. And in the fourth watch of the night Jesus went unto them, walking on the sea. And when the disciples saw him walking on the sea, they were troubled, saying, It is a spirit; and they cried out for fear. But straightway Jesus spake unto them, saying, Be of good cheer; it is I; be not afraid (Matthew 14:22-27; also Mark 6:46-51; John 6:16-21).

Analysis and Word Study

22. *Constrained. (enagkasen)*. It means literally "compelled" or "forced." This word is also in Luke 14:23. The crowd became excited and wanted to seize Jesus by force and to make him king. This act would have resulted in a political revolution and would defeat all the plans of Jesus about His kingdom. It is possible the disciples were influenced by the crowd and Jesus decided to send them away in the boat to better deal with the others.[1]

23. *Into the mountain (eis to oros)*. After the crowd was dismissed Jesus went up alone into the mountain on the eastern side of the lake to pray. He felt the need to communicate with the Father at a time when the disciples misunderstood Him and the people wanted to mislead Him.

47

24. *Tossed with waves.* A sudden and violent squall arose that was characteristic of that inland sea, surrounded with mountain gorges.[2]

25. *Walking on the sea (peripaton epi ten thalassan).* A nature miracle by our Lord where He walked on the water to reach the disciples in the ship.

26. *They were troubled (etarachthesan).* These men were really "terrified" when they saw Jesus walking on the sea. They thought they were witnessing an apparition *(phantasma),* "ghost," or "specter" from *phantazo,* coming from *phaino.* They were filled with fear over this event.[3]

27. *Be of good cheer.* The word cheer *(tharseo)* means to be of good courage. Courage and confidence should be the attitude.[4]

Interpretation and Application

All three of the Gospel accounts agree that this miracle in connection with the feeding of the five thousand occurred on the evening of the same day. Jesus asked His disciples to enter the ship. When we compare the accounts, we discover, as mentioned before, that the multitude wanted to force Jesus into being a king. So He left them and retreated to a mountain to be alone.[5]

Jesus continually withdrew from the crowd, even from His own friends, to be alone with the Father. It was His means of having intimate communication with the Father. What an important truth that is for each of us today.

We tend to live, move, and have our being in relation to others. We are constantly in a crowd. Our modern world seems to live in a crowd. The atmosphere of the crowd is always one of hurry, restlessness, and confusion. The media complete the cycle of activity for most days that include time spent at home and work.

We lose the capacity for solitude. It makes us feel awkward and uncomfortable. We become companions to others and strangers to ourselves. Many people dread the quiet stillness and cannot stand to be alone with themselves, let alone with God. We have surely lost the value and meaning of being in the presence of our Lord. Many blessings await those who would follow the example of Jesus in withdrawing to pray.

This cogent truth finds emphasis in the realm of spiritual experiences. Many moments of vision and understanding have occurred in the quiet hours. Jacob was alone at Bethel when he dreamed of the ladder stretching from heaven to earth. He was alone at Peniel when, in a chance character-changing encounter, he beheld the "face of God." Moses was alone in the wilderness when the bush began to burn, and he met God, the Great I AM. The writer of Psalm 46 recognized the spiritual value of solitude when he wrote, "Be still and know that I am God." The impact that Jesus makes on the world can still be measured by the frequency with which He withdrew to the mountain or wilderness to spend time in prayer. The very reason Jesus could walk on the water is that He prayed on the earth.

There can be no truly monumental or deep spiritual life unless we shut out the world to be shut in with God. We live in a world that is full of God. In the quiet moments He draws nearest to us.[6]

Jesus knew all about the disciples' dilemma. He was aware they were in the boat having a rough time. He realized He would soon be joining them on the water.

He understands all about you, too. He senses the trouble you are going through, empathizes with your problems and your difficulties, and comes to you in the midst of them.

He frightened the disciples when He walked to them on the water between 3 and 6 in the morning as they strained at the oars against a head wind. It is a typical picture of our own human struggles without the presence and power of Christ.[7]

They thought they were seeing a ghost, an apparition. Their peril turned to panic. They were more worried about what they saw walking on the waves than the waves themselves. We do rush into terror, feel frightened by a shadow, threatened by harmless activity. We are often on edge about all kinds of worries and imagined perplexities. If we had more faith, we would not be nervous wrecks but would acknowledge who is in control of our lives. The dreaded ghost would vanish and instead of a terrible experience we would hear His words: "Be of good cheer; it is I; be not afraid" (Matt. 14:27). This is the ever-recurring message of our Lord to our hearts: "Be of good cheer; it is I; be not afraid." If it could only stick and stay, instead of constantly slipping away, our peace would be lasting.

It is like the experience of Peter. He wanted to do what Jesus did. He wanted to be where Jesus was. Peter *did* walk on the water for a short time until his faith faltered. We can see from the experience of Peter's joining Jesus on the water that we, too, can become a part of the miraculous handiwork of God.

How many of us have this sort of courage to face such a challenge? Are we willing to give up our earthbound security and commit ourselves to Him? Are we prepared to leave the familiar to face the unknown?

Jesus asked Peter to "come." He did not object to Peter's sharing in the miraculous. What is the abiding secret to spiritual success? It is seen so vividly in this incident. Peter stepped down out of the boat. "He walked on the water, to go to Jesus." "But ... when he saw the wind boisterous, he was afraid; and beginning to sink, he cried, saying, Lord, save me." Jesus reached out His hand, caught him, and scolded him with, "O thou of little faith, wherefore didst thou doubt?"

If we would live close enough to Jesus, and could keep our eyes on Him in faith and trust, we would not sink so often when waves of life beset us. We would, instead, be like the eye of the hurricane. Surrounded by all kinds of external trouble, we would nonetheless be at peace within.

10

A FAITH REWARDED
The Syrophenician's Daughter

Then Jesus went thence, and departed into the coasts of Tyre and Sidon. And, behold, a woman of Canaan came out of the same coasts, and cried unto him, saying, Have mercy on me, O Lord, thou son of David; my daughter is grievously vexed with a devil. But he answered her not a word. And his disciples came and besought him, saying, Send her away; for she crieth after us. But he answered and said, I am not sent but unto the lost sheep of the house of Israel. Then came she and worshipped him, saying, Lord, help me. But he answered and said, It is not meet to take the children's bread, and to cast it to dogs. And she said, Truth, Lord: yet the dogs eat of the crumbs which fall from their masters' table. Then Jesus answered and said unto her, O woman, great is thy faith: be it unto thee even as thou wilt. And her daughter was made whole from that very hour (Matthew 15:21-28; also Mark 7:24-30).

Analysis and Word Study

22. *A Canaanitish woman. (gune Chananaia).* The Phoenicians were descended from the Canaanites, the original inhabitants of Palestine. They were of the Semitic race, even though pagan.[1]

23. *For she crieth after us.* The disciples disliked this activity of a strange woman crying after them.

24. *I am not sent.* Jesus assumed a new approach with this woman of Phoenicia. She, in a way, represents the problem of the Gentile world. He calls the Jews "the lost sheep of the house of Israel" regardless of the conduct of the Pharisees.[2]

26. *It is not meet to take the children's bread, and to cast it to dogs.* It was a term of reproach. Paul called the Judaizers dogs when he wrote "Beware of the dogs" (Phil. 3:2). The word Jesus used was *kunarion*, "a little dog." He was following the policy of the Jew first and then the Gentile. The Jews were the chosen channel through whom God had elected to reach the Gentiles. Jesus used the illustration of the children of the household at the table and their little pets under the table. He taught that it was proper for the children to be fed first, then the little dogs, their pets.[3]

27. *Even the dogs (kai ta kunaria).* She was not offended at the implication of being a Gentile dog. She accepted the use of the word and turned it to her own advantage, for the little dogs eat of the crumbs (*psichion*, little morsels) that fall from the table of their masters.

28. *As thou wilt.* The faith of the woman made it possible for her daughter to be healed.[4]

Interpretation and Application

Tyre and Sidon were cities of Phoenicia, and Phoenicia was a part of Syria. Phoenicia was situated between Galilee and the sea coast. Tyre was forty miles northwest of Capernaum. It was one of the extraordinary natural harbors of the world from earliest times. Sidon was twenty-six miles northeast of Tyre, and sixty miles north of Capernaum. The Phoenician cities were all independent and were rivals. The Phoenician sailors will always be famous as the men who first found their way by following the stars.

The amazing fact is that Jesus was in Gentile territory. There are several reasons why Jesus may have ventured into that area. He may have wanted to give an indication that the Gentiles would have a place in the kingdom of God. He may have gone there because He was under attack from so many in His own country. He had been branded a sinner by the scribes and Pharisees because He broke their rules and regulations. Herod considered Him a menace, and the people of Nazareth had treated Him with dislike.[5]

The woman came to Jesus and begged for her daughter, who was troubled with a demon, to be healed. Jesus did not speak to her at first. His silence would seem for the moment to mean refusal. The disciples spoke out that she was troublesome because "she crieth after us."

It is somewhat unusual for Jesus to refuse to answer the cry and plea of anyone. There is a mystery and an answer in the silences of Jesus.

This case of the Canaanitish woman with a sick daughter seemed the kind that would appeal to the Christ who went about doing good. She had gone beyond the race barrier. She recognized how a Jew was hesitant to ask and unlikely to receive anything from a Gentile. But she, a Gentile, was asking a tremendous request of a Jew, and not merely for herself but for another, her daughter. It seems that her motive behind it all was her unselfish love of a mother.

This is how the disciples felt. Their words indicate more than a dismissal. They imply a granting of her desire.[6]

Jesus, however, was silent at her initial request. She seemed to have proof of her earnestness and faith. When Jesus speaks, He gives us a clue to His silence. His mission was to the Jews, not the Gentiles.

The woman persisted by imploring, "Lord, help me." But He answered, "It is not meet to take the children's bread, and to cast it to dogs" (Matt. 15:26).

The dog was not then what it is today. The dog, to the Greek, meant a shameless and audacious woman. It was also a term of contempt to the Jew. The word, however, used by Jesus, described not a wild dog of the streets but a pet dog of the house. Jesus removed the sting from the word with His voice while leaving the truth intact.

The woman could have walked away by then feeling rejected and disappointed. She could, but she didn't. Instead she replied: "Truth, Lord: yet the dogs eat of the crumbs, which fall from their master's table" (Matt. 15:27). Here is the secret to the healing of her daughter. She would not take no for an answer but persisted in her petition to the Lord. The word *no* turned around spells *on*. She kept on asking until her request was granted.

"Then Jesus answered and said unto her, O woman, great is thy faith: be it unto thee even as thou wilt. And her daughter was made whole from that very hour" (Matt. 15:28).

She was doing what Christ taught us to do. Keep on praying and asking God for what you need. His parables teach perseverance in our plea for His help.

11
THE GREAT CATCH
Draught of Fishes

After these things Jesus shewed himself again to the disciples at the sea of Tiberias; and on this wise shewed he himself. There were together Simon Peter, and Thomas called Didymus, and Nathanael of Cana in Galilee, and the sons of Zebedee, and two other of his disciples. Simon Peter saith unto them, I go a fishing. They say unto him, We also go with thee. They went forth, and entered into a ship immediately; and that night they caught nothing. But when the morning was now come, Jesus stood on the shore: but the disciples knew not that it was Jesus. Then Jesus saith unto them, Children, have ye any meat? They answered him, No. And he said unto them, Cast the net on the right side of the ship, and ye shall find. They cast therefore, and now they were not able to draw it for the multitude of fishes. Therefore that disciple who Jesus loved saith unto Peter, It is the Lord. Now when Simon Peter heard that it was the Lord, he girt his fisher's coat unto him. (for he was naked,) and did cast himself into the sea. And the other disciples came in a little ship; (for they were not far from land, but as it were two hundred cubits,) dragging the net with fishes. As soon then as they were come to land, they saw a fire of coals there, and fish laid thereon, and bread. Jesus saith unto them, Bring of the fish which ye have now caught. Simon Peter went up, and drew the net to land full of great fishes, an hundred and fifty and three: and for all there were so many, yet was not the net broken (John 21:1-11; also Luke 5:1-11).

Analysis and Word Study

1. *Shewed.* The meaning is deeper than appearing. It occurs frequently in the New Testament referring to God and Christ. The appearing is addressed to spiritual perception, and suggests a spiritual effect. [1]

2. *There were together.* These seven (Peter, Thomas, Nathanael, the sons of Zebedee, and two others). The sons of Zebedee were James and John (Matt. 4:21).

3. *I go a fishing.* Peter had been a fisherman by trade and they were probably waiting in Galilee for a meeting with Christ. The others were ready to do the same. The fishing trip was unsuccessful.

4. *When day was now breaking.* It was dark but the dawn was beginning to appear. Jesus came to the beach and stood there. [2]

5. *Children (Paida).* The word used by Jesus in speaking to His men. It is an expression like "my boys."

6. *The right side.* Jesus knew where the fish were. The picture here is of the disciples tugging at the net that was so full of fishes.

7. *It is the Lord.* Peter put on the upper garment worn by fishers over his waistcloth and tucked it under his girdle. He did this after John recognized Jesus. [3]

8. *A little ship.* This little boat was probably not another boat accompanying the vessel.

Two hundred cubits. A little over a hundred yards.

9. *They were come to land.* Those in the boat came ashore. [4]

11. *Full of great fishes, an hundred and fifty and three*: All authorities agree to the abundance of fish in the Sea of Galilee. The number stated indicates the possibility that the fish were actually counted. The great fishes *(megalon)* "large" might be contrasted with the small fish found in the lake. [5]

Interpretation and Application

There are two accounts in the Gospels of the miraculous catch of fish. One transpired before the resurrection and the other afterwards.

The Sea of Galilee must have been crowded with shipping. It was also one of the best fishing spots available.

The most common net, the net which was cast, was like a circular cone of fine mesh. The open circular edge of the cone was weighted with pellets of lead all around. The net was skillfully and adroitly cast into the sea and drawn toward the fisherman. The fish were caught in the cone, and the mesh was too fine for them to escape.

There are certain kinds of fishing always carried out at night—an unusual sight. With a blazing torch, the boat would glide over the flashing sea, and the men would stand gazing keenly into it until their prey was sighted. Quick as lightning, they would fling their net or throw their spear. Often, tired fishermen would come sullenly into harbor in the morning, having toiled all night without a catch.[6]

Peter and his friends had been fishing all night but without success. Jesus was teaching on the shore of the lake, and the people crowded about Him. In order to have more room to speak, He stepped into one of the boats and asked Peter to move it away from land. When Jesus finished teaching the people He asked Peter to let the nets down for a catch.

Peter did not believe there were any fish available for catching because he had been fishing all night. However, he did what Jesus requested him to do and caught so many fish the net broke. They had to seek help from their partners in the other boat.

In 1875 people laughed at the idea of putting a telegraphic cable between England and America. A team of scientists felt that it could be done. The line broke on several occasions. The next year they tried it again with a different method. The lines again broke, and they abandoned the attempt. Finally, after several tries failed, an expedition succeeded, and on August 5, 1878, communication between England and the U.S. occurred across the ocean, because someone refused to accept failure as final.

Kepler, the first of the modern astronomers, spent seventeen years in study and research and tested no less than nineteen different theories before he succeeded in discovering the explanation of the movements of the earth and other planets in their motion around the sun.[7]

Jesus was constantly challenging people to do the impossible.

The reaction of Peter to this miracle was to fall down at Jesus' knees. He felt humbled by it all. "When Simon Peter saw it, he fell down at Jesus' knees, saying, Depart from me; for I am a sinful man, O Lord. For he was astonished, and all that were with him, at the draught of the fishes which they had taken: And so was also James, and John, the sons of Zebedee, which were partners with Simon. And Jesus said unto Simon, Fear not; from henceforth thou shalt catch men. And when they had brought their ships to land, they forsook all, and followed him" (Luke 5:8-11).

It is arresting that God chose fishermen to do the work of the kingdom. A disciple, because he is a disciple, cannot understand everything about his Master. These men were humble enough to be taught and simple enough to learn. The disciple is a man who paraphrases sentences, obscures mysteries, complicates what is clear, multiplies difficulties, magnifies non-essentials, weakens the essential, and doubts too often.

A prophet suffers without these men and also suffers with them. Jesus realized He needed men to continue His words and work on earth. So He chose them. A Galilean, he chose them from among the Galileans. A poor man, He chose them from among the poor; a simple man, He called simple men whose simplicity made them receptive.

He did not choose them from the rich, because riches made them less dependent upon God. He did not choose them from among the scribes and Pharisees, because they were more tied to their law than to the Lord.

He knew these men were rough but full of integrity, were ignorant but ardent, and that He could in the end mold and shape them into the Master's men. How He did it is a miracle itself.[8]

The account of the fishing miracle in the Gospel of John is quite similar. After His resurrection, the Lord appeared one morning, on the shore of the lake, to several of the disciples, who had again been fishing all night without a catch. He instructed them again to cast their net, and they were not able to draw it for the multitude of fishes.

"Simon Peter went up, and drew the net to land full of great fishes, an hundred and fifty and three: and for all there were so many, yet was not the net broken. Jesus saith unto them, Come and dine.

And none of the disciples durst ask him, Who art thou? knowing that it was the Lord" (John 21:11-12).

The One who calls us to be "fishers of men" also provides His men with fish. The resources of God are always adequate to meet our needs in abundance.

12

A CRIPPLE CURED
An Impotent Man Healed

After this there was a feast of the Jews; and Jesus went up to Jerusalem. Now there is at Jerusalem by the sheep market a pool, which is called in the Hebrew tongue Bethesda, having five porches. In these lay a great multitude of impotent folk, of blind, halt, withered, waiting for the moving of the water. For an angel went down at a certain season into the pool, and troubled the water: whosoever then first after the troubling of the water stepped in was made whole of whatsoever disease he had. And a certain man was there, which had an infirmity thirty and eight years. When Jesus saw him lie, and knew that he had been now a long time in that case, he saith unto him, Wilt thou be made whole? The impotent man answered him, Sir, I have no man, when the water is troubled to put me into the pool: but while I am coming another steppeth down before me. Jesus saith unto him, Rise, take up thy bed, and walk. And immediately the man was made whole, and took up his bed, and walked: and on the same day was the sabbath (John 5:1-9).

Analysis and Word Study

1. *A feast of the Jews.* It cannot be determined exactly what feast it was. It has been identified with the Passover, Pentecost, and the Feast of Tabernacles.[1]

2. *By the sheep market a pool.* The word means "pertaining to sheep." The gate was near the temple on the east of the city. The word for pool is found only in this chapter and John 9:7,11 in the New Testament. It was a diving or swimming pool.[2]

Having five porches. Stoa was a covered colonnade where people could gather. Some have felt this was the Pool of Siloam (9:7), even though John distinguishes them.

4. *Troubled the water.* This verse is lacking in the oldest and best manuscripts like Aleph BCDW 33 Old Syriac, Coptic versions, Latin Vulgate. It is probably added to make the statement in verse 7 clearer. The Jews explained the healing virtues of the intermittent spring by the ministry of angels.[3]

5. *An infirmity thirty and eight years.* Literally "having spent thirty and eight years."

6. *Knew that he had been a long time.* We don't know exactly how Jesus fathomed this, whether by observation, overhearing people talk, or by supernatural knowledge.

7. *When the water is troubled.* There was a popular belief that, at each outflow of this spring, there was healing power in the water for the first one getting in.[4]

8. *Arise, take up thy bed, and walk.* This was a sort of exclamation like our "Get up." It means to pick up the pallet and then "go on walking."

9. *Took up his bed and walked.* He took it up at once and continued to walk. The man was healed on the sabbath. This became the first of the violations of the Jewish sabbath rules by Jesus in Jerusalem that led to considerable controversy and bitterness.[5]

Interpretation and Application

There were three Jewish feasts called "feasts of obligation." Every adult male Jew who lived within twenty miles of Jerusalem was obligated to attend. These were the Feast of Pentecost, the Feast of the Passover, and the Feast of Tabernacles. We are not sure which feast it was at the time this miracle occurred. It was most likely either the Feast of Passover or of Pentecost. The Passover was in mid-April, and Pentecost was seven weeks later. Jesus always attended the feasts because He delighted in worship with His own people.

Apparently, Jesus was alone at the time since no mention is made of the disciples. He came to a certain pool whose location was uncertain. It may have been near either the Sheep Market or the

Sheep Gate. The name of the pool was Bethesda which could mean "The House of Mercy." The Greek word used is *kolumbethra*, which comes from the verb *kolumban*, "to dive."[6] The pool was deep enough to dive into and to swim in. In fact, there was a subterranean spring beneath it which every now and then caused water to bubble up. The people believed that the bubbling up was caused by an angel, and that the person who succeeded in being first into the pool after the water was disturbed would be cured of whatever sickness he had.

In Jesus' time every Jew had a real belief in angels. Jesus, however, did not discuss this with the man at the pool but went directly to his need. Frank Laubach, the literacy missionary servant of Christ, observed: "It would be better for us to throw away ninety-nine percent of our learning and of our tangled philosophy and stick to just one simple thing for our daily life, to keep asking God, 'Who needs me next, Father?' "

The Bible reports that there were five porches at Bethesda. Recent excavations have confirmed this. There are two separate pools that are surrounded by a porch on all sides with one porch separating the two pools, making a total of five. The pool, discovered within the last few years, is exactly as it is described in John.[7]

The Bible describes it as being full of sick people. "In these lay a great multitude of impotent folk, of blind, halt, withered, waiting for the moving of the water. And a certain man was there, which had an infirmity thirty and eight years" (John 5:3,5).

It does not matter what the trouble is, Jesus can cure it. If there is a habit that has gripped us to the extent that it seems impossible to break, Jesus can enable us to break it. If there is an obsession too hard to stop, Jesus can help us do it. If we have a pernicious fear, Jesus can enable us to conquer it.

Jesus asked the man a piercing question: "Do you want to get well?" Any psychologist will tell us that many people prefer to keep their illnesses rather than to be cured of them.

There was a girl named Kathleen G. She was about twenty, young and healthy, and a typist living in a certain small town. She became engaged to the Episcopal priest of the village and was very happy. She had an elated feeling of importance, but her fiance broke off the engagement. From that time Kathleen developed certain symptoms. One was no appetite. She began to lose weight and became pale, thin, and anemic. Every doctor she visited insisted: "She must eat." Finally she was carried to a psychologist who discovered that subconsciously she wanted to starve to death. She was seeking revenge on her ex-fiance by starving herself to death. She did not want to recover. The psychological treatment she received helped her discover the truth and enabled her to be cured.[8]

This can even happen from lesser circumstances. A morning before an engagement we do not want to keep, we develop a headache. Maybe we are facing an unwanted encounter or a guest that causes us to have an upset stomach. Illness can be an escape. It can elicit sympathy and attention that we otherwise would not have received.

Some people live in a pool of self-pity. Life has dealt them a hard blow. The circumstances they are going through are too much for them. It is always someone else's fault.

"The impotent man answered him, Sir, I have no man, when the water is troubled, to put me into the pool: but while I am coming, another steppeth down before me" (John 5:7).

This man considered himself an innocent victim, taken advantage of by others—like the person who is treated wrongly by his associates at work, his wife, or his friends. He explained, "No one would put me in the water." Self-pity keeps us from seeing ourselves as responsible for our condition. Therefore, it can become a comfortable outlet because the responsibility for action is shifted to someone else.

Depression and self-pity can destroy us. It is a dangerous and difficult world in which to live. It would be much better to leave this bed of misery and find meaning to life.

"Jesus saith unto him, 'Rise, take up thy bed, and walk.' And immediately the man was made whole, and took up his bed, and walked: and on the same day was the sabbath" (John 5:8-9).

Jesus challenged him to do the impossible. We must cooperate with the Lord for our healing. Jesus could heal Him, but He could not get up and do the man's walking for him. When Jesus is behind the effort the impossible becomes possible!

13
DELIVERED FROM DEATH
Raising of Lazarus

Now a certain man was sick, named Lazarus, of Bethany, the town of Mary and her sister Martha. (It was that Mary which anointed the Lord with ointment, and wiped his feet with her hair, whose brother Lazarus was sick.) Therefore his sisters sent unto him, saying, Lord, behold, he whom thou lovest is sick. When Jesus heard that, he said, This sickness is not unto death, but for the glory of God, that the Son of God might be glorified thereby. Now Jesus loved Martha, and her sister, and Lazarus. When he had heard therefore that he was sick, he abode two days still in the same place where he was. Then after that saith he to his disciples, Let us go into Judaea again. His disciples say unto him, Master, the Jews of late sought to stone thee; and goest thou thither again? Jesus answered, Are there not twelve hours in the day? If any man walk in the day, he stumbleth not, because he seeth the light of this world. But if a man walk in the night, he stumbleth, because there is no light in him. These things said he: and after that he saith unto them, Our friend Lazarus sleepeth; but I go, that I may awake him out of sleep. Then said his disciples, Lord, if he sleep, he shall do well. Howbeit Jesus spake of his death: but they thought that he had spoken of taking of rest in sleep. Then said Jesus unto them plainly, Lazarus is dead. And I am glad for your sakes that I was not there, to the intent ye may believe; nevertheless let us go unto him. Then said Thomas, which is called Didymus, unto his fellow disciples, Let us also go, that we may die with him. Then when Jesus came, he found that he had lain in the grave four days already. Now Bethany was nigh unto

Jerusalem, about fifteen furlongs off: And many of the Jews came to Martha and Mary, to comfort them concerning their brother. Then Martha, as soon as she heard that Jesus was coming, went and met him: but Mary sat still in the house. Then said Martha unto Jesus, Lord, if thou hadst been here, my brother had not died. But I know, that even now, whatsoever thou wilt ask of God, God will give it thee. Jesus saith unto her, Thy brother shall rise again. Martha saith unto him, I know that he shall rise again in the resurrection at the last day. Jesus said unto her, I am the resurrection, and the life: he that believeth in me, though he were dead, yet shall he live: And whosoever liveth and believeth in me shall never die. Believest thou this? She saith unto him, Yea, Lord: I believe that thou art the Christ, the Son of God, which should come into the world. And when she had so said, she went her way, and called Mary her sister secretly, saying, The Master is come, and calleth for thee. As soon as she heard that, she arose quickly, and came unto him. Now Jesus was not yet come into the town, but was in that place where Martha met him. The Jews then which were with her in the house, and comforted her, when they saw Mary, that she rose up hastily and went out, followed her, saying, She goeth unto the grave to weep there. Then when Mary was come where Jesus was, and saw him, she fell down at his feet, saying unto him, Lord, if thou hadst been here, my brother had not died. When Jesus therefore saw her weeping, and the Jews also weeping which came with her, he groaned in the spirit, and was troubled, And said, Where have ye laid him? They said unto him, Lord, come and see. Jesus wept. Then said the Jews, Behold how he loved him! And some of them said, Could not this man, which opened the eyes of the blind, have caused that even this man should not have died? Jesus therefore again groaning in himself cometh to the grave. It was a cave, and a stone lay upon it. Jesus said, Take ye away the stone. Martha, the sister of him that was dead, saith unto him, Lord, by this time he stinketh: for he hath been dead four days. Jesus saith unto her, Said I not unto thee, that, if thou wouldest believe, thou shouldest see the glory of God? Then they took away the stone from the place where the dead was laid. And Jesus lifted up his eyes, and said, Father, I thank thee that thou hast heard me. And I knew that thou hearest me always: but because of the people which stand by I said it, that they may believe that thou hast sent me. And when he thus had spoken, he cried with a loud voice, Lazarus, come forth. And he that was dead came forth, bound hand and foot with graveclothes: and his face was bound about with a napkin. Jesus saith unto them, Loose him, and let him go. Then many of the Jews which came to Mary, and had seen the things which Jesus did, believed on him. But some of them went their ways to the Pharisees, and told them what things Jesus had done (John 11:1-46).

Analysis and Word Study

1. *Was sick named Lazarus, of Bethany.* This Bethany is about two miles (11:18) east of Jerusalem on the southeast slope of Olivet and is now called El Azariyeh, from the name Lazarus. The two sisters are named for further identification of Lazarus. Martha was apparently the elder sister (11:5,19).[1]

2. *It was that Mary which anointed the Lord with ointment, and wiped his feet with her hair.* The description here is added to make plainer who Mary was. There is an evident anticipatory allusion to the incident described by John in 12:1-8. The effort to link Mary of Bethany with Mary Magdalene and then both names with the sinful woman of Luke 7:36-50 is cruel to the memory of both Mary of Bethany and Mary Magdalene. We have two different women under different circumstances doing a similar act for utterly different purposes.[2]

3. *Thou lovest.* There was no invitation for Jesus to come. The news about Lazarus was sufficient.

4. *Unto death.* It was not to have death as its final issue.[3]

But for the glory of God. The death of Lazarus would illustrate God's glory. The raising of Lazarus from the tomb would bring glory to the Son of God.

5. *Now Jesus loved (agape de).* The sisters expected him to come at once and to heal Lazarus.

6. *In the same place where He was.* It was long enough for Lazarus to die.

9. *In the day.* It was a twelve-hour day in contrast with the twelve hours of night. Jesus had courage to face His enemies again in order to do the Father's will about Lazarus.

11. *Sleepeth.* This was common as a metaphor for death like our cemetery.[4]

14. *Plainly (parresiai)*—is dead. It means "died."

15. *For your sakes that I was not there.* Why? That they may witness his raising from the grave. This would help their belief concerning Jesus.[5]

17. *Had lain in the grave four days already.* He had been four days in the tomb.

18. *Fifteen furlongs.* About two miles.[6]

22. *Wilt ask of God.* The verb denotes the asking of an inferior from a superior. (The idea of thinking of Jesus as a prophet — "an inferior position.")

25. *I am the resurrection and the life.* They were not mere doctrines about future events but present realities in Jesus Himself. Jesus had taught the future resurrection often (6:39), but here He meant more, even that Lazarus is now alive.[7]

27. *The Son of God, which should come into the world.* One of the offices of Christ the Messiah was, according to Jewish expectations, to raise the dead, and thus, confessing Him to be the Christ, she implicitly confessed Him also to be the quickener of the dead.

28. *Master.* This was a name, probably the name, whereby the Lord was known in the innermost circle of His own (Matt. 23:8; John 20:16; 13:13).[8]

30. *Now Jesus was not yet come into the town.* Martha had her interview while He was still coming and left Him to hurry to Mary with the news.

32. *Fell down at his feet. (epesen autou pros tous podas).* She said what Martha had said to Jesus (verse 21), but she said no more—only wept (verse 33).[9]

33. *Groaned in the spirit.* (*enebrimesato toi pneumati*). The word for "groaned" occurs three times elsewhere. In every case it expresses a charge, or remonstrance, accompanied with a feeling of displeasure. Some explain the feeling as indignation at the hypocritical mourning of the Jews, or at their unbelief and the sisters' misapprehension; others as indignation at the temporary triumph of Satan, who had the power of death.[10]

35. *Jesus wept* (*edakrusen ho Iesous*). (Ingressive first aorist active indicative of *dakruo*, old verb from *dakru* or *dakruon*, a "tear" (Acts 20:19), only here in the New Testament.) It never means to wait. It represents a possible reaction from the strain in verse 33, but primarily it was the human sympathy of His heart with Martha and Mary touched with the deep feeling of their need. This is the shortest verse in the Bible, but no other verse carries more meaning in it.[11]

39. *Take ye away the stone* (*arate ton lithon*). They could handle this much without the exercise of Christ's divine power.

He stinketh. (*ede ozei*). It means to give out an odor. Lazarus had been dead for four days.

41. *Father, I thank thee.* Jesus had prayed to the Father concerning the raising of Lazarus. He had the answer before He acted.

42. *And I knew* (*ego de eidein*). This kind of confident knowledge was no new experience with Jesus. It had "always" (*pantote*) been so.

43. *He cried with a loud voice, Lazarus, come forth.* The loud voice was not for the benefit of Lazarus, but for the sake of the crowd standing around that they might see that Lazarus came forth simultaneously with His command.[12]

44. *He that was dead came forth* (*exelthen ho telhnekos*). He came out of the tomb with his grave clothes. His legs were probably bound separately.

45. *Believed on him* (*episteusan eis auton*). This was another occasion where those who experienced the miracles of Jesus believed on Him.

46. *Went away to the Pharisees* (*apelthon pros tous Pharisaious*). Some did not have the courage to break away from the rabbis. It was a crisis for the Sanhedrin.[13]

Interpretation and Application

Jesus was well aware Lazarus was dying. He stayed where He was until he died because He had a much greater blessing in mind.

Jesus often visited the home of Mary, Martha, and Lazarus at Bethany. They were close friends. Jesus loved them, and they loved Him in return. This is why it was so difficult for Mary and Martha to understand why Jesus did not come to Lazarus when he became ill.

Jesus had explained to His disciples, "Our friend Lazarus sleepeth; but I go, that I may awake him out of sleep" (John 11:11). This puzzled the disciples, but the Bible spoke of sleep in reference to death. It relates in the case of Stephen's martyrdom that he "fell asleep" (Acts 7:60). Paul wrote of those who "sleep in Jesus" (1 Thess. 4:13). Jesus plainly stated that Lazarus was dead.

Jesus was cognizant that raising Lazarus from death would seal His fate with the Jewish authorities. I heard a story of a lifeboat service. There was a terrible storm. A ship was driven onto the rocks, and the lifeboat was called out. A younger member of the crew was afraid. He looked at the raging sea and remarked to one of the older members of the crew: "If we go out into that sea, we will never get back alive." The older man, answered: "Son, we've gotta go out; but we don't have to come back."[14]

Jesus set out for Bethany. When news reached Martha that He had arrived, she virtually wept, "Lord, if thou hadst been here, my brother had not died" (John 11:21). He then assured her, "Thy brother shall rise again" (John 11:23). Martha replied that she believed he would rise again in the last day. Jesus answered her, "I am the resurrection, and the life: he that believeth in me, though he were dead, yet shall he live: And whosoever liveth and believeth in me shall never die. Believest thou this? She saith unto him, 'Yea, Lord: I believe that thou art the Christ, the Son of God, which should come into the world' " (John 11:25-27).

Later Jesus wept at the grave of Lazarus. Death nearly always brings an abundance of sorrow and crying. We can look forward to the day described in the Book of Revelation. "And God shall wipe away all tears from their eyes; and there shall be no more death, neither sorrow, nor crying, neither shall there be any more pain: for the former things are passed away" (Rev. 21:4). Jesus fulfilled the truth of this when He raised Lazarus from the grave.

Christ commanded them. "Take ye away the stone" (John 11:39). He could have moved the stone with a command, but He wanted them to do their part. Prayer and effort go together for a miracle.[15]

"Then they took away the stone from the place where the dead was laid. And Jesus lifted up His eyes, and said, Father, I thank thee that thou hast heard me. And I knew that thou hearest me always: but because of the people which stand by I said it, that they may believe that thou hast sent me. And when he thus had spoken, he cried with a loud voice, Lazarus, come forth. And he that was dead came forth, bound hand and foot with graveclothes: and his face was bound about with a napkin. Jesus saith unto them, Loose him, and let him go" (John 11:41-44).

Jesus was not putting on an act for a beautiful stained-glass window; He was calling a soul and spirit back into a body. He was not giving poetry for the demythologizers; He was giving an order to be obeyed. No ministerial effort ever totally satisfies those at a graveyard. All they want is to be reunited with their loved one.[16]

Lazarus came back to life again. They returned to the house. Martha prepared dinner for them, and the man returned to life from death ate with his sisters and his friends. Mary was not able to take her eyes away from the conqueror of death, who, having wiped the tears from His eyes, ate and drank as if this day were like any other day.

The reaction to such a miracle by others follows the same pattern. Many believed on Jesus when they saw what He did. However, His enemies, those vipers full of jealous venom, planned for His death. There are many people today who would do away with Jesus. He is all right in a manger scene, on a stained-glass window, or some other location. However, His words and His teaching, when they interfere with the life-style of those who prefer sin to righteousness, who would rather "live it up" than to live in Him, who follow the world instead of God, would prefer not to see Him killed, *but simply ignored.*

However, the words of the One who declared — "I am the resurrection, and the life: he that believeth in me, though he were dead, yet shall he live: And whosoever liveth and believeth in me shall never die. Believest thou this?" (John 11:25)—are still true.

Jesus raised three people from the dead during His life on earth. He did this to comfort the sorrow of those who loved the dead, to console a mother, a father, two sisters. Two of these resurrections were in public; one, that of the daughter of Jairus, was accomplished in the presence of very few, and Jesus asked them to keep quiet about it.

It is significant to remember that Jesus spoke to the dead person as if he were not dead but only asleep. He said, as to a child oversleeping, "Young man, I say unto thee, arise." When they told Him that the daughter of Jairus was dead, He answered, "Weep not, she is not dead but sleepeth." When they told the news of the death of Lazarus, He said, "He is not dead but sleepeth." He awakened people from the experience of death. Death for Him was only a sleep, a deeper sleep than the common sleep of everyday experience. It became a sleep broken by a supernatural love. It was the love of one whose tears flow at the sight of others' tears and who wishes to relieve the sorrow.[17]

Jesus understands our sorrow. We must remember that Jesus knows completely about the future life. If we knew as much about it as Jesus does, we would rejoice when a saved loved one enters into it.

"But as it is written, Eye hath not seen, nor ear heard, neither have entered into the heart of man, the things which God hath prepared for them that love him" (1 Cor. 2:9).

One of the great blessings for the Christian is being reunited with redeemed loved ones who have died. We can look forward to this family reunion in heaven.[18]

We will have a spiritual body in heaven instead of our physical body. "In the resurrection they neither marry, nor are given in marriage, but are as the angels of God in heaven" (Matt. 22:30).[19]

The most important miracle of all is the miracle of eternal life. Jesus Christ is the Son of God. He came to forgive us of our sins. He died on the cross so we could live forever. Ask God for forgiveness of sin, repent, and ask Jesus to save you. This miracle lasts forever.

Conclusion

The miracles of Jesus are for today and for you. Contrary to what some have written, taught, or preached, there is nothing in the New Testament that states the miracles of Jesus ceased with His departure from this earth.

Scoffers have sneered, "I don't believe that Jesus is alive." The other person replies: "Well, that's strange, I was just talking with Him." In the same way, I know personally that Jesus' miracles have occurred in my life and in the lives of others. I share these experiences with you only to encourage you to believe God for anything—also to show His power, exalt His name, and bring glory to Him.

Over the years, I have seen God demonstrate His almighty strength and power by using miracles associated with the weather.

When I left for my first revival trip outside the United States in Guatemala City, Central America, I didn't know it would be a trip that included some unusual miracles.

I was to preach for two weeks. The first week went well with good attendance at the church. However, there were no decisions for salvation made during the services.

I was staying in a hotel during the first week of the revival meeting. My schedule consisted of getting up by 7 A.M., getting dressed, and eating breakfast alone. That was an interesting experience in itself because the menu was in Spanish, and the waiter did not speak English.

I spent from 8 A.M. until the missionary picked me up at noon in prayer. I also read the Bible during this time. There was some time spent studying the message for the evening service, but mostly it was time in prayer. I have always believed, and still do, that no work of God, and especially no great accomplishment for God, occurs apart from a tremendous amount of praying. This fact is evident in the life of Jesus because He spent so much of His time in prayer. It is very important to realize that if anyone could have accomplished a lot with little prayer, it should have been Jesus ... He was God and without sin. Yet, Jesus would spend hours at a time praying. He would pray late into the night. He would rise up early before daylight to pray. The Bible records that He prayed all night before He chose His twelve apostles.

I was praying in my room in the afternoon. It was during the rainy season, and it had rained every day for the past week. While I was praying, God spoke to my mind and told me to go to the window. I got off my knees and went to the window. As I looked out the window, the Lord said, "What do you see?" I replied, "Rain." He then said, "I want you to pray in the service tonight that the rain would stop as a sign that people should receive me as their Savior and Lord and be saved." (Most of the congregation were professing believers, but some were not Christians.)

My first thoughts were, *Am I hearing correctly? Is this the Lord telling me to do this?*

I returned to praying again and had not been praying very long before I heard the words again. "Go to the window." I went to the window a second time, and He said, "What do you see?" and I replied, "Rain." Then the same message came that I heard before to pray in the service tonight that the rain would stop as a sign for people to be saved.

I continued praying, and a third time the words came to me, "Go to the window." I went to the window, and He said, "What do you see?" I said, "I see rain." Then He repeated for the third time that I should pray in the service tonight for the rain to stop for people to accept Jesus and be saved. The same words were used each time.

Well, after experiencing this for three consecutive times, I felt convinced that it was the Lord who was telling me to do this.

So I shared all this with the missionary who interpreted for me in the services as I preached. The people spoke Spanish, and I was not fluent enough in their language to use it in my preaching.

So I began my message that evening by praying this prayer out loud, "Lord, I ask you to stop the rain as a sign that the lost people would receive Jesus Christ as their personal Savior and Lord and be saved." Then I preached.

It was still raining when I returned to my hotel room that night. I was thinking—*Have I made a fool of myself?* The next morning the rain had stopped. There were a couple of times during the second week that the weather was cloudy, and one night there was thunder, but it didn't rain and when I boarded my plane for the flight home the sun was shining.

There were some people who accepted Christ during the second week as a result of the weather miracle. One of them was a fine young man who was in the local university studying to be an engineer. The missionary told me he was very intelligent and had great hopes for the Lord to use him. He felt that the young man would have much influence on others.

I received a letter from the missionary stating that the day after I left Guatemala City it rained. It was amazing to me that God had stopped the rain in a city with over 500,000 population for a few people to be saved in a small mission church of 100 people.

The greatest miracle of all is the salvation of the person who repents of his sin and receives Jesus Christ into his heart and is "born again."

During my ministry, there was another time that God stopped the rain. We were having a county-wide revival in a tent in which all the Baptist churches were participating. It had been raining almost every day since the meeting began, and the rain was keeping some of the people away because of the mud. I was praying at the church where I was pastor in Macon, Mississippi, and the Lord spoke to me and told me to pray in the service that night that the rain would stop. The circumstances of this meeting and God's command were similar to my previous experience in Guatemala City, even though I was not the evangelist. However, in order to pray, the person leading the service would have to call on me. I was in charge of the counseling for the crusade. I said, "Lord, if you want me to pray this prayer tonight, I will know if the person in charge calls on me to pray." I didn't tell anyone about this. I was sitting on the platform that night with the other pastors when I was asked to pray. So I obeyed and prayed that the rain would stop and for God to bless the meeting. The rain stopped that night, and it didn't rain anymore during the meeting, and it helped the attendance to improve. Strangely enough, the next night during the service the same thunder and lightning came—but no rain. To God be the glory!

A third miracle about weather occurred during the time I was pastoring a church in Memphis, Tennessee. It had not rained during the summertime for over two months, and the drought was a problem. The Lord told me to pray for rain during the morning service on Sunday. It started raining that afternoon.

My personal spiritual philosophy is to be open and receptive at all times to whatever the Holy Spirit wants to do in and through you. Also, since God knows everything and has all wisdom, knowledge, and power He knows what is best in every circumstance. The Holy Spirit is a person. Therefore, He hears you when you pray and will speak to you when you listen. It would be a strange relationship always to be talking to someone and never hear them speak to you.

I find a vacuum in many Christians today. They rely on the Bible (God's inspired, infallible Word) to speak to them (which they should) but fail to allow the Holy Spirit to do so. God the Father and Jesus His Son are in heaven, but the Holy Spirit is the One who lives within the heart of each Christian.

Every Christian should have a close, intimate relationship with the Holy Spirit. The Bible gives us many truths to live by but does not give us specific information about certain directions and guidelines for decisions and actions that need to be taken from time to time.

Someone may say that God gives us a mind to use—and He does—but His wisdom is greater than ours. Therefore, we need to be constantly asking the Holy Spirit for information, instruction, and help for everything we do.

I believe we should take all important matters to God. A person should consult God about the more serious decisions that affect the rest of their lives. Matters such as a college major, marriage, career, and jobs should be lifted up for an answer.

If family and close friends are willing to give advice, why not God? Especially since He knows the future.

God wants to hear about our smallest problems. For instance, as I have traveled to work on the interstate and cars began to back up, I consult the Holy Spirit on my travel course.

In my home city of Memphis, Tennessee, crimes are committed frequently. Several in my family have been robbed. So if I have to use an automatic teller I talk to the Lord before I go to the machine.

God loves you and wants what is best for you in the little things and the big things. He cares about what happens to you. You may wonder, *How do you hear from God?* You don't hear your heartbeat with your physical ears unless you use a stethoscope. It is inside you beating silently. Well, how do you hear from anybody? You listen for them to speak to you. God usually speaks silently to the mind and heart of people instead of out loud. The Holy Spirit is "in us."

If you have not experienced God speaking to you, then ask Him to start doing this, keep on asking, and be receptive to hearing Him.

Someone has concluded that Jesus spent three-fourths of His ministry healing people. I have experienced His healing power and seen others healed too. The Bible says "Jesus Christ the same, yesterday, and today, and forever" (Hebrews 13:8). Jesus uses doctors, hospitals, medicine, etc., to bring healing today. He can also use His own power.

Have you ever heard anyone pray, "Lord, if it be Your will, please heal a certain person". Of course, it is always correct to ask for God's will, but if you determine His will ahead of time, you can more easily believe and ask specifically for absolute healing. Do you ever pray, "Lord, if it is your will, please save this person"?

Jesus never refused to heal anyone in the New Testament that came to Him for healing. "And, behold, there came a leper and worshipped him, saying, Lord, if thou wilt, thou canst make me clean. And Jesus put forth his hand, and touched him, saying, I will; be thou clean. And immediately his leprosy was cleansed." (Matthew 8:2-3). There is only one case where Jesus almost refused to heal (Mark 7:25-30).

Jesus represented the perfect example of the Father. Jesus never made anyone sick. He did constantly heal people. If it was the Father's will for people to be sick then Jesus would have been working against the Father's will when He healed.

When Jesus referred to the spiritual source of people's sickness, disease, or infirmities, He always related it to the devil. Therefore, Jesus eliminated what the devil had created. A few years ago, I had an infection, and the doctor gave me an antibiotic to clear it up. I kept taking the medicine for seven months. During this time I was praying for healing, but it didn't come. The doctor recommended surgery. I asked him for a few days to decide. I then continued to pray for healing, but this time I sought the Lord aggressively for healing and begged Him to clear up the infection to avoid surgery. When I returned to the doctor he examined me and replied, "The infection's gone." He seemed surprised and asked me what happened. I told him, "I prayed very hard for healing, and God was good to grant it."

Death can provide healing, too. Our first child was a girl who was born healthy. Our second child was a girl who was born with Spina Bifida. We named her Helen Ruth. She had an open spine, could not make a sound when she cried, and required oxygen to keep breathing. The day she was being transported by ambulance to Memphis, Tennessee, from Meridian, Mississippi, I was left alone with her, and she was in the ambulance without oxygen. She began to turn blue, and I didn't know what to do except pray for help. I turned to my right, and there was the doctor who delivered her. He immediately came and with one finger helped her start breathing again. By that time, they arrived with her oxygen for the trip to Memphis.

One night my wife and I were at home where I was pastoring a church in Mississippi. We had some slide pictures of Helen Ruth we were looking at, and I went up to one of them and touched her on the screen and said to Charlene, "Let's believe God for a miracle of healing for Helen Ruth." We prayed and during the night the phone rang. It was my parents in Memphis calling to tell us Helen Ruth had died. We wanted her to be healed for earth, but God chose to heal her for heaven.

I was preaching in a meeting up in the mountains of Japan. There were several churches participating together. One afternoon I was visiting with one of the pastors. We visited with a young lady who was not saved and when I shared the gospel with her she opened her heart and invited Jesus in. This is a miracle because Japanese people are very, very slow to accept Western religions. They hold to their customs and traditions. They become outcast most of the time if they become Christians.

We also visited with a man who was deaf in one ear. He asked me to pray for his hearing problem. I laid my hand on his ear and prayed for him. As I prayed, I felt something move inside his ear. When I took my hand away, the man said, "I can hear." There was great rejoicing over those two miracles of our Lord that afternoon.

I thank God for His miracle power. I cannot understand or explain why everyone who prays for healing is not healed. The example of Jesus shows He is for people being well and healthy.

All things are possible with God. I was on an air flight from Albuquerque, New Mexico, to Denver, Colorado, with a connecting flight to Memphis. There was bad weather at the Denver airport, and a delay caused me to miss my flight to Memphis.

When I checked with the airline's customer service they rescheduled me on a flight the following day through Chicago with a two-hour wait there. I asked about a flight on another carrier. The agents said they would not honor the ticket because it was a frequent-flyer ticket. Naturally, I was praying about all of this so I decided to check with another carrier anyhow. The agent was very nice and did not hesitate to give me a ticket for a direct flight the next morning to Memphis. There were no evening flights to Memphis on either airline. The next need was a hotel room for the evening. I didn't anticipate this to be a problem so I went to one of the hotels at the airport. They said all the rooms were taken, and all the airport hotels were too. Well, I called anyway, and the hotel said, "We have one room left," and I said, "I'll take it!" When the shuttle bus came to get me the driver said, "Right after you called, four people asked for a room." The Lord had answered my prayer.

Suppose you pray and believe but nothing happens. Keep on praying and believing. Jesus taught perseverance in prayer. I have a personal formula: Pray, believe, and trust. We need to be open and receptive to all God has for us. We sometimes put roadblocks in the way that keep us from experiencing the blessings of the Lord. The Bible says, "We have not because we ask not." Jesus taught us to "ask and receive."

Jesus never taught us to doubt. He never taught us to fear or be afraid. We should all have a proper fear of God in the sense of His holiness. But Jesus was always telling us to "not be afraid," "have faith," "only believe," etc. His example was one of faith. We should think in faith, look in faith, talk in faith, and walk in faith. Faith is very important in receiving miracles. Does this mean that imperfect faith keeps God from answering prayer? Of course not. One person responded to Jesus, "I believe, help my unbelief." Jesus granted his request. But Jesus always encouraged people to believe in Him personally to meet their needs.

Some people today, unfortunately, do not ask God for or expect miracles from God. For instance, if a person has a terminal illness and the doctor says, "I'm sorry I cannot help you," many people give up hope. The Lord knows what He is doing, and He always knows what is best for His children. Jesus is not only your Lord and Savior, but also your friend. As your friend, He loves you and cares about your need. Let's take your special need to the Lord right now. Ask the Holy Spirit right now for His miracle power to meet your need or someone else's need.

Dear Lord, You know all about the need expressed by Your child. Please answer this need by Your miraculous power and by Your will. In Jesus' Name. Amen.

I would love to hear from you about how God answered this prayer. Let us rejoice together as we experience the miracles of Jesus.

82

Footnotes

Introduction

[1]William Barclay, *The Mind of Jesus* (New York: Harper and Row, 1961), 66.

[2]*Encyclopaedia Britannica*, Volume 12 (Chicago: Benton Publishers, 1980), 275.

[3]Barclay, Ibid. 67.

[4]Ethelbert Stauffer, *Jesus and His Story* (New York: Alfred A. Knopf, 1960), 8.

[5]Barclay, Ibid., 67.

Chapter 1

[1]A. T. Robertson, *Word Pictures in the New Testament* (Nashville, TN: Broadman Press, 1932), 33.

[2]Marvin R. Vincent, *Word Studies in the New Testament* (New York: Charles Scribner's Sons, 1918), 79.

[3]Robertson, Ibid., 33.

[4]Ibid.

[5]Vincent, Ibid., 79.

[6]R. C. Trench, *Notes on the Miracles of our Lord* (Grand Rapids: Baker Book House, 1949), 63.

[7]Vincent, Ibid., 80.

[8]Robertson, Ibid., 34.

[9]William Barclay, *The Bible Study Series*, Gospel of John, Vol. 1. (Philadelphia: Westminster Press, 1956).

[10]Vincent, Ibid., 80.

[11]Ibid

[12]Trench, Ibid., 66.

[13]Vincent, Ibid., 80.

[14]Robertson, Ibid., 35.

[15]Ibid.

[16]Ibid.

[17]Vincent, Ibid., 81.

[18]Robertson, Ibid., 36.

[19]Ibid.

[20]Trench, Ibid., 69.

[21]Robertson, Ibid., 36.

[22]Ibid., 37.

[23]Vincent, Ibid., 83.

[24]*Encyclopaedia Britannica* (Chicago: Benton Publishers, 1980), Volume 19, 875-881.

[25]William Barclay, *And He Had Compassion* (Valley Forge: Judson Press, 1976), 156-157.

[26]Giovanni Papini, *Life of Christ* (New York: Dell Publishing Co., 1951), 175.

[27]Trench, Ibid., 66.

[28]Papini, Ibid., 178.

Chapter 2

[1]A. T. Robertson, *Word Pictures in the New Testament* (Nashville: Broadman Press, 1932), 227.

[2]W. E. Vine, *An Expository Dictionary of New Testament Words* (Old Tappan, NJ: Fleming H. Revell Co., 1966), 330.

[3]Robertson, Ibid., 330.

[4]R. C. Trench, *Notes on the Miracles of Our Lord* (Grand Rapids: Baker Book House, 1949), 210.

[5]Ibid., 211.

[6]Ibid.

[7]Vine, Ibid., 80

[8]Trench, Ibid., 211.

[9]David A. Redding, *The Miracles of Christ* (New York: Harper and Row, 1964), 75.

[10]William Barclay, *And He Had Compassion* (Valley Forge: Judson Press, 1976), 31-35.

[11]Ibid., 36.

[12]Redding, Ibid., 77.

[13]Charles L. Allen, *The Touch of the Master's Hand* (Westwood, NJ: Fleming H. Revell Co., 1956), 34-38.

Chapter 3

[1]Alfred Edersheim, *The Life and Times of Jesus the Messiah* (Grand Rapids: Eerdmans Co., 1979), 542-545.

[2]A. T. Robertson, *Word Pictures in the New Testament* (Nashville: Broadman Press, 1932), 64.

[3]Ibid., 65.

[4]William Barclay, *And He had Compassion* (Valley Forge: Judson Press, 1976), 132-133.

[5]Ibid., 135.

[6]Ibid., 141.

[7]Ibid., 143.

[8]Charles L. Allen, *The Touch of the Master's Hand* (Westwood, NJ: Fleming H. Revell Co., 1956), 50.

Chapter 4

[1]Kenneth S. Wuest, *Wuest's Word Studies* (Grand Rapids, MI: Eerdmans Publishing Co., 1978), 109.

[2]Ibid., 109.

[3]A. T. Robertson, *Word Pictures in the New Testament* (Nashville, TN: Broadman Press, 1930), 299.

[4]Ibid., 300.

[5]Ibid.

[6]Wuest, Ibid., 113.

[7]William Barclay, *And He Had Compassion* (Valley Forge, PA: Judson Press, 1976), 46-47.

[8]David A. Redding, *The Miracles of Christ* (New York: Harper and Row, 1964), 87-88.

[9]Barclay, Ibid., 51.

[10]George MacDonald, *The Miracles of Our Lord* (Wheaton, IL: Shaw Publishers, 1980), 54.

[11]Arnold Prater, *Miracle Living* (Irvine: Harvest House Publishers, 1978), 14.

[12]R. C. Trench, *Notes on the Miracles of Our Lord* (Grand Rapids: Baker Book House, 1949), 117.

Chapter 5

[1]Kenneth S. Wuest, *Wuest's Word Studies, Mark* (Grand Rapids, MI: Eerdmans Publishing Co., 1978), 36.

[2]Ibid., 36.

[3]A. T. Robertson, *Word Pictures in the New Testament* (Nashville, TN: Broadman Press, 1930), 66.

[4]Wuest, Ibid., 37.

[5]David A. Redding, *The Miracles of Christ* (New York: Harper and Row, 1964), 83-84.

[6]William Barclay, *The Daily Study Bible, the Gospel of Mark* (Philadelphia: The Westminster Press, 1946), 28-30.

[7]George MacDonald, *The Miracles of Our Lord* (Wheaton: Shaw Publishers, 1980), 54.

[8]Barclay, Ibid., 30.

[9]Hastings, Ibid., 257.

Chapter 6

[1]W. E. Vine, *An Expository Dictionary of New Testament Words* (Old Tappan, NJ: Fleming H. Revell Co., 1966), 113.

[2]A. T. Robertson, *Word Pictures in the New Testament* (Nashville, TN: Broadman Press, 1930), 68.

[3]R. C. Trench, *Notes on the Miracles of Our Lord* (Grand Rapids, MI: Baker Book House, 1949), 90.

[4]Ibid., 91.

[5]Robertson, Ibid., 69.

[6]James and Edward Hastings, *The Speaker's Bible*—Vol. 2 (Grand Rapids: Baker Book House, 1971), 3-4.

[7]Clifton J. Allen, *The Broadman Bible Commentary*, Vol. 9, Luke-John (Nashville: Broadman Press, 1970), 75.

[8]Robertson, Ibid., 69.

[9]Trench, Ibid., 66.

[10]Hastings, Ibid., 134.

Chapter 7

[1]A. T. Robertson, *Word Pictures in the New Testament* (Nashville, TN: Broadman Press, 1930), 294.

[2]Kenneth S. Wuest, *Wuest's Word Studies* (Grand Rapids, MI: Eerdmans Publishing Co., 1978), 101.

[3]Robertson, Ibid., 295.

[4]Ibid., 296.

[5]Wuest, Ibid., 105-106.

[6]Robertson, Ibid., 297.

[7]William Barclay, *And He Had Compassion* (Valley Forge, PA: Judson Press, 1976), 53-55.

[8]James and Edward Hastings, *The Speaker's Bible*, Vol. 2 (Grand Rapids, MI: Baker Book House, 1971), 6-7.

[9]Giovanni Papini, *Life of Christ* (New York: Dell Publishing Co., 1951), 134.

[10]Barclay, Ibid., 58-59.

[11]R. C. Trench, *Notes on the Miracles of Our Lord* (Grand Rapids, MI: Baker Book House, 1949), 101.

Chapter 8

[1]A. T. Robertson, *Word Pictures in the New Testament* (Nashville, TN: Broadman Press, 1930), 96.

[2]Ibid., 96-97.

[3]Marvin Vincent, *Word Studies in the New Testament* (New York: Charles Scribner's Sons, 1918), 144-145.

[4]Robertson, Ibid., 99-100.

[5]Charles L. Allen, *The Touch of the Master's Hand* (Westwood, NJ: Fleming H. Revell Co., 1956), 121.

[6]Ibid., 122.

[7]Ibid., 125-126.

Chapter 9

[1] A. T. Robertson, *Word Pictures in the New Testament* (Nashville, TN: Broadman Press, 1930), 118.

[2] R. C. Trench, *Notes on the Miracles of Our Lord* (Grand Rapids, MI: Baker Book House, 1949), 89.

[3] Robertson, Ibid., 119.

[4] W. E. Vine, *An Expository Dictionary of New Testament Words* (Old Tappan, NJ: Fleming H. Revell Co., 1966), 184.

[5] Trench, Ibid., 173.

[6] James and Edward Hastings, *The Speaker's Bible*, Vol. 1 (Grand Rapids, MI: Baker Book House, 1971), 218-219.

[7] David A. Redding, *The Miracles of Christ* (New York: Harper and Row, 1964), 23-26.

Chapter 10

[1] A. T. Robertson, *Word Pictures in the New Testament* (Nashville, TN: Broadman Press, 1930), 125.

[2] Ibid., 125.

[3] Kenneth S. Wuest, *Wuest's Word Studies* (Grand Rapids, MI: Eerdmans Publishing Co., 1978), 152.

[4] Robertson, Ibid., 125.

[5] William Barclay, *The Daily Study Bible*, Gospel of Mark (Philadelphia, PA: The Westminster Press, 1956), 179-181.

[6] James and Edward Hastings, *The Speaker's Bible*, Volume 1 (Grand Rapids, MI: Baker Book House, 1971), 230.

Chapter 11

[1] Marvin Vincent, *Word Studies in the New Testament* (New York: Charles Scribner's Sons, 1918), 295.

[2] A. T. Robertson, *Word Pictures in the New Testament* (Nashville, TN: Broadman Press, 1930), 318.

[3] Ibid., 319.

[4] Vincent, Ibid. 297-298.

[5] Ibid., 298.

[6] William Barclay, *And He Had Compassion* (Valley Forge, PA: Judson Press, 1976), 126.

[7] Ibid., 127.

[8] Giovanni Papini, *Life of Christ* (New York: Dell Publishing Co., 1951), 216-218.

Chapter 12

[1] A. T. Robertson, *Word Pictures in the New Testament*. (Nashville, TN: Broadman Press, 1930), 78.

[2]Marvin Vincent, *Word Studies in the New Testament* (New York: Charles Scribner's Sons, 1918), 131.

[3]Robertson, Ibid., 79.

[4]Ibid., 80.

[5]William Barclay, *And He had Compassion* (Valley Forge: Judson Press, 1976), 172.

[6]Ibid., 175.

[7]James H. Bailey, *The Miracles of Jesus for Today* (Nashville, TN: Abingdon, 1977), 55.

[8]Barclay, Ibid., 177.

Chapter 13

[1] A. T. Robertson, *Word Pictures in the New Testament* (Nashville, TN: Broadman Press, 1930), 192.

[2]Ibid., 193.

[3]Marvin Vincent, *Word Studies in the New Testament* (New York: Charles Scribner's Sons, 1918), 200.

[4]Robertson, Ibid., 195, 196.

[5]Ibid., 196.

[6]Vincent, Ibid., 201.

[7]Robertson, Ibid., 199.

[8]R. C. Trench, *Notes on the Miracles of Our Lord* (Grand Rapids: Baker Book House, 1979), 255, 256.

[9]Robertson, Ibid., 201.

[10]Vincent, Ibid., 204.

[11]Robertson, Ibid., 203.

[12]Ibid., 206.

[13]Ibid., 207.

[14]William Barclay, *And He Had Compassion* (Valley Forge, PA: Judson Press, 1976), 199.

[15]Charles L. Allen, *The Touch of the Master's Hand* (Westwood, NJ: Fleming H. Revell Co., 1956), 50.

[16]David A. Redding, *The Miracles of Christ* (New York: Harper and Row, 1964), 175.

[17]Giovanni Papini, *Life of Christ* (New York: Dell Publishing Co., 1951), 174-175.

[18]Allen, Ibid., 149-151.

[19]Ibid., 152.

Bibliography

Allen, Charles L. *The Touch of the Master's Hand.* Westwood, NJ: Fleming H. Revell Co., 1956.

Allen, Clifton J. *The Broadman Bible Commentary.* Nashville, TN: Broadman Press, 1969.

Bailey, James H. *The Miracles of Jesus for Today.* Nashville, TN: Abingdon Press, 1977.

Barclay, William. *The Daily Study Bible Series.* Philadelphia, PA: The Westminster Press., 1959.

Dufour, Leon. *Dictionary of Biblical Theology.* New York: Desclee Co., 1967.

Edersheim, Alfred. *The Life and Times of Jesus the Messiah.* Grand Rapids, MI: Zondervan Publishing House, 1955.

Encyclopaedia Britannica. Chicago: Benton Publishers, 1980.

Guignebert, Charles. *Jesus.* New York: University Books, 1956.

Habershon, Ada R. *The Study of the Miracles.* London: Morgan and Scott. n.d.

Hastings, Edward. *The Speaker's Bible.* Grand Rapids, MI: Baker Book House, 1978.

Holy Bible. Philadelphia, PA: A. J. Holman Co.

Jeremias, Joachim. *Jerusalem in the Time of Jesus.* Philadelphia, PA: Fortress Press, 1969.

Keller, Ernst and Marie-Louise. *Miracles in Dispute.* Philadelphia, PA: Fortress Press, 1969.

Lockyer, Herbert. *All the Miracles of the Bible.* Grand Rapids, MI: Zondervan Publishing House, 1961.

MacDonald, George. *The Miracles of Our Lord.* Wheaton, IL: Harold Shaw Publishers, 1980.

Miller, Madeleine S. and J. Lane. *Encyclopedia of Bible Life.* New York: Harper and Brothers Publishers, 1955.

Moule, Charles F. D. *Miracles.* London: A. R. Mowbray and Co., 1965.

Orr, James. *The International Standard Bible Encyclopaedia.* Chicago: The Howard-Severance Co., 1915.

Papini, Giovanni. *Life of Christ.* New York: Dell Publishing Co., 1957.

Redding, David A. *The Miracles of Christ.* New York: Harper and Row Publishers, 1964.

Robertson, A. T. *Word Pictures in the New Testament.* Nashville, TN: Broadman Press, 1930.

Salstrand, George. *What Jesus Began: The Life and Ministry of Christ*. Nashville, TN: Broadman Press, 1976.

Schaaffs, Werner. *Theology, Physics, and Miracles*. Washington, D.C.: Canon Press, 1974.

Spurgeon, Charles H. *Spurgeon's Expository Encyclopedia*. Grand Rapids, MI: Baker Book House, 1978.

Stauffer, Ethelbert. *Jesus and His Story*. New York: Alfred A. Knopf, 1960.

Trench, R. C., *Notes on the Miracles of our Lord*. Grand Rapids, MI: Baker Book House, 1949.

Unger, Merrill. *Principles of Expository Preaching*. Grand Rapids, MI: Zondervan Publishing House, 1955.

Vincent, Marvin, R. *Word Studies in the New Testament*. New York: Charles Scribner's Sons, 1918.

Vine, W. E. *An Expository Dictionary of New Testament Words*. Old Tappan, NJ: Fleming Revell Co., 1966.

Wuest, Kenneth S. *Word Studies*. Grand Rapids, MI: Eerdmans Publishing Co., 1950